Normandy
Coast

Andrew Sanger

Credits

Footprint credits
Editor: Ria Gane
Production and layout: Emma Bryers
Maps: Kevin Feeney
Cover: Pepi Bluck

Publisher: Patrick Dawson
Managing Editor: Felicity Laughton
Advertising: Elizabeth Taylor
Sales and marketing: Kirsty Holmes

Photography credits
Front cover: Teo Nuvoli/Shutterstock.com
Back cover: DOPhoto/Shutterstock.com

Printed in the United States of America

Publishing information
Footprint *Focus Normandy Coast*
1st edition
© Footprint Handbooks Ltd
February 2013

ISBN: 978 1 908206 97 8
CIP DATA: A catalogue record for this book
is available from the British Library

® Footprint Handbooks and the Footprint
mark are a registered trademark of
Footprint Handbooks Ltd

Published by Footprint
6 Riverside Court
Lower Bristol Road
Bath BA2 3DZ, UK
T +44 (0)1225 469141
F +44 (0)1225 469461
footprinttravelguides.com

Distributed in the USA by Globe Pequot
Press, Guilford, Connecticut

The content of Footprint *Focus Normandy
Coast* has been taken directly from
Footprint's *Normandy* guide which was
researched and written by Andrew Sanger.

Every effort has been made to ensure that
the facts in this guidebook are accurate.
However, travellers should still obtain advice
from consulates, airlines, etc, about travel
and visa requirements before travelling.
The authors and publishers cannot accept
responsibility for any loss, injury or
inconvenience however caused.

3923

Contents

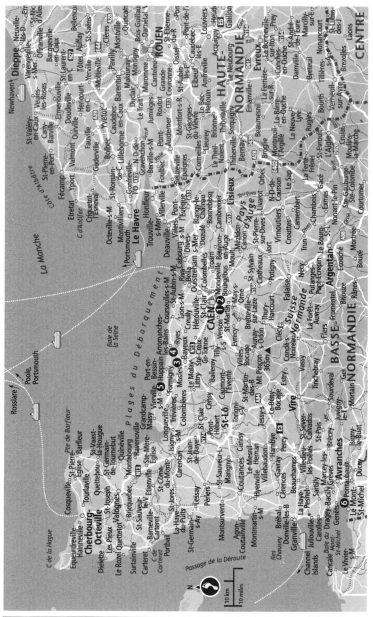

4 ● Normandy Coast

Ever since Vikings arrived on its shores in the ninth century, the sea has dominated Normandy's destiny and its character. The Norse raiders made themselves at home, and eventually were even given a duchy to call their own, but continued to live close to the waterfront, building a string of harbours still in use today.

Under the Dukes of Normandy, their descendants established themselves as the greatest of seafarers and sailors, explorers and colonists – and fighters. Not the least of them was William the Bastard, Duke of Normandy, who sailed across the Channel and became William the Conqueror, King of England (as recorded on the famous tapestry displayed at Bayeux).

Throughout the Middle Ages, the Normans carried their art and architecture, religion and culture, planting it everywhere from Ireland to the Holy Land.

The duchy became tranquil, rustic and prosperous. Such a richly productive territory gave rise to Normandy's long tradition of hearty, flavoursome cooking served in generous quantities – still very much enjoyed today. Its seaside became a place of elegant beach resorts and Impressionist art.

But then war came to Normandy again. The duchy's beaches, during the 1944 Liberation of France, once more determined its fate and the destiny of Europe. The coastal areas, especially, preserve the memory of those days. In the struggle, some fine historic towns were badly damaged but fortunately others escaped, and much has been restored, including some of France's loveliest Gothic masterpieces.

Today, Normandy conveys a deep peace and contentment. The city of Caen manages to be both modern and medieval. Along the wartime Landing Beaches, evocative memorials recall the sacrifice and drama of that time. Once-grand holiday resorts retain something of their old elegance and charm. In between all these sights are Normandy's small, simple fishing harbours and a seashore of wild cliffs and gentle beaches.

Planning your trip

Places to visit on the Normandy Coast

Whether you arrive in Normandy from the sea at Dieppe, Le Havre or Cherbourg-Octeville, or by road from Paris or the Channel Tunnel, you will experience the contrasting faces of the region.

Normandy is large, and varies hugely across its range. Indeed, the old duchy is big enough that administratively it is not one region, but two: Haute Normandie (Upper Normandy) and Basse Normandie (Lower Normandy). Even within Lower Normandy there are striking contrasts, as it reaches from its capital, the Conqueror's city of Caen, down the maritime Cotentin Peninsula, to dramatic Mont-St-Michel abbey rising pyramid-like from sea-washed sands.

Caen and the Landing Beaches
At the centre of Normandy's broad spread, the *département* of Calvados seems to conjure all that's most evocative of the duchy. It extends from a long Channel coastline of wartime Landing Beaches and attractive old harbours like Honfleur or the belle epoque resorts of the Côte Fleurie, to fine historic towns like Bayeux and the thriving capital Caen. Inland is exquisite old-fashioned countryside like the apples-and-cream Pays d'Auge with its half-timbered manor houses. Calvados produces some of Normandy's most famous products, and gives its own name to a refined but fiery apple brandy drunk as a digestif. The farms and dairies of Calvados put several other familiar names on the gourmet table, including most of the region's strong, creamy cheeses, and its high-quality milk, crème fraîche and butter.

Cotentin and Mont-St-Michel
Despite the ferry traffic passing through its largest town, the busy port of Cherbourg-Octeville, Normandy's westerly *département* of Manche remains probably the least known region in Normandy. It is dominated by the distinctive character of the Cotentin Peninsula, projecting granite headlands far into the English Channel (*La Manche* in French), but this is no wilderness. The region was densely populated in ancient times, and put up the strongest resistance to Roman rule. It was the first part of Normandy to be settled by the invading Norsemen. In the Middle Ages, too, it prospered. Today it preserves a powerful sense of history, with some of the finest Norman churches, a rustic hinterland of fields, woodland and hedges and many distinctively Viking place names. Heading south, the steep, wild and rocky coast gives way to many little harbours and long sandy beaches, with a string of traditional family resorts like Carteret and Granville.

At its foot, the Cotentin Peninsula skirts the edge of evocative Mont-St-Michel Bay. this southern corner of Normandy is one of the most visited places in France: the abbey of Le Mont-St-Michel, rising spectacularly from the seawaters and tidal marshes where Normandy touches Brittany.

Dieppe to Le Havre
Upper Normandy is made up of the *départements* of Seine-Maritime, which climbs from the right bank of the River Seine, and Eure, most of which lies on the left bank. Through the middle of the region flows the wide river itself, making its way to the sea in great

Don't miss...

meandering twists and turns that end in a vast estuary overlooked by the city of Le Havre. North of the river, Upper Normandy meets the English Channel in lofty white cliffs – strangely sculpted by the wind and waves – and sandy beaches, and bustling towns like the popular port and market-town of Dieppe and the charming Alabaster Coast.

Best of the Normandy Coast

St Etienne Church, Abbaye aux Hommes, Caen
Combining the simple lines of the original Norman Romanesque with a superb and delicate Norman Gothic reconstruction, the majestic and serene church of the Mens' Abbey – built by William the Conqueror, and where he was buried – puts it among the world's greatest architectural achievements. See page 27.

Le Mémorial de Caen
An ambitious, dignified museum encompassing the whole subject of the Second World War: how it happened, its horrors and outcome, displaying a vast amount of astonishing original material ranging from a letter from Albert Einstein to President Roosevelt, to uniforms and newsreels, tanks and equipment. See page 28.

Caen market
The city's main Sunday market is a huge, colourful, vibrant gathering along the marina quayside where you can choose not just the finest products of the Calvados coast and countryside, but also browse fascinating sections devoted to hats and clothes, shoes, carpets, toys and a multitude of arts and crafts. See page 33.

Honfleur harbour
Brimming with charm, Honfleur's historic fortified Vieux Bassin wowed the Impressionists as it does artists today. Bars and art galleries line the cobbled quays and picturesque lanes lead to enchanting museums, including one devoted to Honfleur-born Impressionist Eugène Boudin and another to local comic artist and composer Erik Satie. See page 36.

Bayeux Tapestry
Surely the most remarkable cartoon strip in history, this 900-year-old embroidery tells the whole story of 1066. Vivid pictures along its 70-m length, captioned in Latin, show the background, the invasion and the outcome of the battle between Normans and Saxons for the crown of England. See page 47.

Arromanches
The little resort of Arromanches-les-Bains, fronting right on to the sand of Gold Beach, is the place to discover what D-Day and the Normandy Landings were about, with its excellent beachfront D-Day Museum, imposing remnants of the Mulberry Harbour still in place and a vivid film reconstruction at Arromanches 360. See page 53.

Normandy American Cemetery, Omaha Beach
The toughest of the Landing Beaches was Omaha, where the Americans lost thousands of men in just hours. They are laid out in this calm, respectful and deeply affecting cemetery beside the beach. The opening and closing scenes of the film *Saving Private Ryan* are set here. See page 55.

Lessay abbey church
This beautifully proportioned little abbey church on the edge of a small country town in the rural Cotentin is one of the best examples of Norman Romanesque architecture: symmetrical, solid and sturdy. Restored after wartime damage using the same stone as the medieval original, it's a haven of tranquillity. See page 73.

Coutances cathedral
One of Normandy's most pleasing examples of Norman Gothic architecture, this huge Cotentin landmark was actually built on to the framework of a much older Romanesque church. The result is an exquisite combination of refined elegance and robust simplicity, with lovely 14th-century sculpture and 13th-century stained glass. See page 78.

Granville
As well as one of western Normandy's best sandy beaches, the Cotentin's main coastal resort has an impressively fortified medieval Upper Town, and fascinating museums ranging from Richard Anacréon's collection of modern art and rare books, to the Christian Dior museum in the designer's childhood home. See page 79.

Le Mont-St-Michel
An ethereal setting between sky and water gives pure magic to this strange abbey-island, reached by a 2-km causeway into the sea. Its stone ramparts are lit up at night, while by day you can climb hundreds of ancient steps on tours of the abbey's evocative churches. See page 84.

Dieppe Market
The crowded, colourful Saturday morning market reaches along Dieppe's Grand'Rue from the busy quayside of the fishing harbour to the heart of the old town, the stalls loaded with cheeses, charcuterie, cider and all the best local produce from Upper Normandy's dairy farms, orchards and fishing boats. See page 96.

Etretat cliffs
A charming little 100-year-old seafront resort built around a medieval core, the real attraction of Etretat is its remarkable 'doorways' carved into white cliffs projecting into the water. Admire them from a beachfront promenade or get a more stirring vista from the green cliff tops that inspired numerous Impressionist painters. See page 101.

St Joseph Church, Le Havre
The very model of Auguste Perret's belief in concrete as the building material of the future, Le Havre's main church is considered the greatest achievement of his post-war reconstruction of the city. Inside, it's a vast space lit by 6500 fragments of coloured glass set into a 110-m spire. See page 106.

Getting to the Normandy Coast

Air
From the UK and Ireland The only international direct flight to Normandy is the one-hour journey from London City airport to Deauville, operated by **CityJet** (cityjet.com). There are one to four departures weekly, with fares from £139 return.

The principal air gateway to Normandy is Paris. There are several flights daily from London Heathrow, London Luton, Edinburgh, most UK regional airports and Dublin, to France's main international airport Charles de Gaulle (CDG), 22 km north of Paris. Less frequent flights depart from London Gatwick and several other UK and Irish local airports, including Cork A small number of flights land at Paris Orly, 15 km south of the capital, most from London City airport. Airlines operating these routes include **Aeromexico, Air Europa, Air France, Air Mauritius, Alitalia, American Airlines, British Airways, Delta Airlines, EasyJet, Flybe, and Qantas.** From Scotland or Ireland **Ryanair** fly to 'Paris' (Beauvais airport, 88 km from Rouen on N31) from Glasgow, Shannon and Dublin.

From North America Several flights depart daily from Chicago, Cincinnati, Detroit, Houston, Los Angeles, Miami, Montreal, New York, Philadelphia, San Francisco, Toronto and Washington DC to Paris Charles de Gaulle, with a less frequent service from Pittsburgh, Salt Lake City, Seattle and Vancouver.

From rest of Europe All European capitals have direct flights to Paris, and there are frequent daily flights to Paris from dozens of other European cities. Within France, internal flights connect French regional airports to Normandy's small airports at Caen, Cherbourg, Deauville, Le Havre and Rouen.

Onward travel from Paris CDG and Orly airports Seven major international car hire companies have desks at the two Paris airports. From Charles de Gaulle to Caen is 255 km via A1 and A13. Alternatively, travel by RER train into central Paris and onward from Paris-St Lazare to Rouen or Caen to reach the Normandy coast.

Rail
Journey time from London St Pancras to Paris Gare du Nord on **Eurostar** ① *T08705-186186, eurostar.com*, is two hours 15 minutes, plus a 30-minute check-in (from £69 return). Eurostar can add onward rail travel to Rouen or Caen. Change in Paris to Paris-St Lazare (allow 1½ hours to change stations) to continue by TGV or intercity rail services to Rouen (journey time from Paris, from one hour 12 minutes, from London four hours 29 minutes, total return fare from London from £89) or Caen (two hours 10 minutes from Paris, five hours 15 minutes from London, total return fare from London from £79).

Rail travel to other destinations on the Normandy coast can be pre-booked with **Rail Europe** ① *T08448-484064, raileurope.co.uk*, in the UK or USA, or the French railway company **SNCF** ① *T08 92 35 35 35, voyages-sncf.com*, from outside France, or within France at any French train station. Catch a train at Paris-St Lazare for Bayeux, Caen, Cherbourg, Deauville, Dieppe, Fécamp or Le Havre. Trains from Paris Montparnasse travel direct to Granville on the Cotentin coast.

Road
Bus/coach Eurolines ① *T0871-781 8181 premium rate, eurolines.co.uk*, run a service from London to Paris, from where you can take a train to Normandy. The journey time is eight to nine hours and while the standard fare is £52, on certain days and times it costs as little as £17 return (including booking fees). Most buses arrive at the station of **Eurolines France** ① *28 av Général-de-Gaulle, Bagnolet, T08 9289 9091, eurolines.fr*, close to the Métro station Gallieni, with a 35-minute onward journey into Paris.

Car The fastest way to travel to Normandy from southeast England is by road and Eurotunnel. **Eurotunnel** ① *T08443-353535, eurotunnel.com*, trains run from the M20 near Folkestone direct to autoroute A16 near Calais. It operates 24 hours a day with up to four departures an hour in peak times. Check-in and departure are rapid, and the crossing takes 35 minutes plus 30 minutes check-in, with little delay in unloading vehicles. Standard fares start from £64 single, £128 return, for a car and up to nine passengers. There are often promotions with lower fares on certain dates, and reductions for frequent travellers, while a five-day return costs £94. The onward driving time into Normandy via autoroutes A16, A28, A29 or A13 is about two hours to Dieppe (180 km) or three hours 15 minutes to Caen (345 km).

Sea
Typical mid-week fares are given below, but look out for frequent bargain special offers. Crossings to Calais, Boulogne or Dunkerque are cheaper.

To Dieppe From Newhaven **LD Lines** ① *T0800-917 1201, ldlines.co.uk*, Monday to Saturday twice daily, crossing time four hours, plus minimum 45-minute check-in, return fare typically £141 for driver and car plus £15 per passenger.

To Le Havre From Portsmouth LD Lines twice daily. One crossing daily. Crossing time 5½ hours by day (on return journey), to eight hours at night (outward journey), plus 45-minute check-in, typical return fare £173 for driver and car, plus around £15 per passenger.

To Caen (Ouistreham) From Portsmouth **Brittany Ferries** ① *T0871-244 0744, brittanyferries.com*, sail three crossings on most days, generally six hours 15 minutes or seven hours 45 minutes overnight crossings, plus 45-minute check-in, typical return fare £250 for car, driver and passenger, £70 return for additional passengers.

To Cherbourg-Octeville From Poole Brittany Ferries sail once daily, four hours 15 minutes, plus 45-minute check-in, typical return fare about £240 for car, driver and passenger, £50 return for additional passengers.
   From Portsmouth Brittany Ferries operate once daily, crossing time three hours, plus 45-minute check-in, typical fare about £380 return for car, driver and passenger, £50 return for additional passengers.

From Rosslare **Irish Ferries** ⓘ *Ireland T0818-300400, irishferries.com*, sail this route. There are about 10 crossings per month, 19- to 20-hour crossing, plus one-hour check-in, typically about €508 return for driver and car, about €50 return per additional passenger, plus compulsory cabin from about €140 return.

To Normandy from the Channel Islands Manche Iles Express ⓘ *Jersey T01534-880756, Guernsey T01481-701316, manche-iles-express.com*, operate seasonal ferry services between the Channel Islands and the Cotentin ports of Diélette, Barneville-Carteret and Granville.

Transport on the Normandy Coast

Rail

French trains are run by the state-owned **SNCF** ⓘ *sncf.com*. As in every other French region, Normandy's principal towns are all connected by fast modern trains several times daily. The main rail routes are Cherbourg-Octeville to Paris (three hours) via Caen (one hour 10 minutes); Caen to Paris (two hours 10 minutes); Caen to Rouen (one hour 35 minutes); Rouen to Paris (from one hour 11 minutes); and Rouen to Le Havre (42 minutes).

Different fares apply depending on the time and day. There are special offers available. For latest fares and departure times, check SNCF's dedicated website for the regions, ter-sncf.com. Remember that on the site, Normandy is two regions: Basse Normandie and Haute Normandie.

Dieppe and Le Havre The national rail company **SNCF** ⓘ *T0825 000276, ter-sncf.com/ haute_normandie*, runs buses (in cooperation with other companies) as well as trains that together provide a good network of regional services between towns in Upper Normandy. Main rail lines from Rouen go to Le Havre (51 minutes) and Dieppe (45 minutes), with changes for other towns, for example Rouen-Fécamp (one change, one hour to one hour 40 minutes). There's a map of the complete SNCF network in Upper Normandy at ter-sncf. com/haute_normandie/carte_horaires/index.asp.

Côte d'Albâtre There is a service between Le Havre and Fécamp (40 minutes).

Calvados There are direct trains between Paris-St Lazare and Caen (two hours 10 minutes) several times daily. There is more than one train an hour between Caen and Bayeux (about 15 minutes), continuing to Cherbourg-Octeville (one hour 10 minutes). There are services from Trouville along the Côte Fleurie to Dives/Cabourg (30 minutes).

Cherbourg-Octeville Regular rail services connect Cherbourg-Octeville to Paris-St Lazare (three hours), via Caen (one hour 10 minutes), and, with one change, to Rennes (three hours 37 minutes) via Coutances (one hour 38 minutes), and, with one or two changes, Granville (about two hours). A TGV service currently connects Cherbourg-Octeville to Dijon via Caen, Roissy and Marne-la-Vallée (Disneyland), but as there is no high-speed line between Roissy and Cherbourg-Octeville, the trains do not travel at TGV speeds and journey times remain unchanged.

Southern Cotentin A direct line connects Granville to Paris Montparnasse (three hours 13 minutes).

Road

Bicycle Picturesque countryside, quiet lanes and gently challenging topography make Normandy a good region for cycling. Long-distance cycle routes include the Voies Vertes (green ways), along former railway lines. A 600 km marked Maritime cycle path along the Normandy coast, taking in Dieppe and the Alabaster Coast, the coast of Calvados and the Landing Beaches, all the way to Cherbourg (and with another section from Coutances to Le Mont St Michel), is under construction, with certain sections already complete.

Local trains within Normandy transport bikes free of charge, without pre-booking, in the luggage compartment.

IGN Cartes de Promenade maps, intended for walkers, are useful. IGN Serie Bleue maps cover a smaller area in more detail. Most tourist offices have information about cycle trails in their area, and can give the addresses of local bike hire firms – usually at least one in every town. Many focus on VTT (mountain bikes) but it is also possible to hire touring bikes. Shop around, as hire fees vary considerably. Expect to pay around €100 a week or €20 a day for a touring bike, or €120 a week, €25 a day, for a mountain bike. Prices for children's bikes are likely to be almost as much.

The city of Caen operates a free bike scheme, V'eol. This gives 30 minutes' free hire, followed by increasing charges for subsequent periods. You have to register for the scheme, and use your credit card to pick up the sturdy roadsters from stands all around town.

Bus/coach Every *département* in Normandy has a local bus network, with timetables geared to the needs of workers and schoolchildren. Most do not cross the *départemental* boundary. Out-of-town sights can be hard to reach by public bus. National rail operator SNCF also runs bus routes to supplement train services; these are shown on railway timetables. There is a flat fare of just €2 for all bus journeys throughout Upper Normandy and Lower Normandy.

There is little public transport between towns along the Côte d'Albâtre between Fécamp, Dieppe and Le Tréport. Regular bus services between Etretat, Fécamp and Le Havre are operated by **Cars Périer** ⓘ *T02 35 46 37 77, cars-perier.com*.

Car Travelling by car makes it easy and enjoyable to explore Normandy's coast. However, with fuel costing about €1.50 per litre, driving has become an expensive option. In addition, traffic congestion, traffic-free streets, and finding somewhere to park all make car travel difficult in larger towns.

Speed limits are generally 110 kph (68 mph) on dual carriageways, and 130 kph (80 mph) on motorways (sometimes lower on toll-free motorways). Otherwise, the maximum speed is generally 50 kph (31 mph) in town, 90 kph (55 mph) out of town. Insurance documents, car registration papers and a full driving licence issued by any EU country or the US must be carried when driving. Third party insurance is compulsory. Comprehensive insurance issued by UK insurers is valid throughout the EU (a so-called Green Card is no longer required). The minimum driving age for a car or motorcycle is 18.

By law you must stop immediately after an accident, with minimum obstruction to traffic. If anyone has been injured, or is under the influence of alcohol, call the police. French motorists must complete an insurance form verifying the facts and all parties must sign to show that they agree that it is a true account. Non-French motorists should exchange details with the other parties. If you break down, put on hazard warning lights (or display a warning triangle).

Misunderstanding this important rule is the main cause of accidents involving foreign motorists in France. Drive on the right *and always give way to anything approaching from the right*, except where signs indicate to the contrary. The main priority signs are a rectangular yellow sign if you have priority, and a yellow rectangle crossed out meaning you no longer have priority. Where two major roads merge, look out for signs showing who has priority (*Vous n'avez pas la priorité* and/or *Cédez le passage*). Two important exceptions are that vehicles emerging from private property don't have priority over traffic on the public highway, and most roundabouts give priority to vehicles already in the roundabout (as in the UK).

Police levy hefty on-the-spot fines for speeding, worn tyres, not wearing a seat belt, not stopping at a Stop sign and overtaking where forbidden. The amount is likely to be €135, but can be considerably more depending on the circumstances. Issuing a receipt is part of the on-the-spot procedure – always be sure to get one, and keep it carefully. Serious violations such as drink driving could lead to your car being impounded, as well as heavy fines or imprisonment.

Service stations, especially on autoroutes, sell a range of excellent road atlases and maps, including the well-respected Michelin and IGN. **Bison Futé** ① *bison-fute. equipement.gouv.fr*, publish an annual map showing less congested itineraries, free from tourist offices and gas stations.

Parking meter charges are relatively modest, but it can be difficult finding a space. Payment is required typically Monday to Friday 0900-1800, Saturday 0900-1200. A good time to find a parking space is lunchtime (1200-1400) and there's often no charge for parking then. Parking spaces painted with blue lines are Zone Bleue, where parking is free for 90 minutes if the time of arrival is displayed in the windscreen with a '*disque horaire pour les zones bleue*', known as a Disque Bleue. Blue EU Disabled Parking photocards issued in the UK are valid in France, but in a Zone Bleue must be used in conjunction with a Disque Bleue.

Car hire is widely available from both international and local firms. At airports, stations and main roads in the cities and resorts you'll see all the familiar car rental names. Prices are generally higher than in other countries, especially for drivers under 25. Before signing the rental agreement, check that any existing damage on a vehicle you are about to rent has been noted. Make sure your rental is for unlimited mileage – some firms may place an upper limit on the free mileage. Be sure to return the car with the same amount of fuel as at the start of the rental, as fuel charges may be imposed by car rental companies.

Where to stay on the Normandy Coast

Chic pre-war resorts, family beach holidays, lively city breaks and simple country living are all among the favourite holiday options here. The Normandy coast is one of the most popular regions in France and appeals to a very wide range of people and interests, with a diverse choice of accommodation to match.

Prices
Most visitors to Normandy are travelling on a package holiday – that is, accommodation and transport (and sometimes meals) combined in an inclusive price, pre-booked with a travel agent or tour operator in their home country. This is normally cheaper and easier than paying for each element of the trip separately. However, package deals usually require a minimum stay of three nights in a hotel, or a week in self-catering or campsite accommodation. You may also be required to arrive at your accommodation on a particular 'changeover day'.

Price codes

Where to stay

€€€€ over €200   €€€ €101-200

€€ €60-100   € under €60

Price codes refer to the cost of a double room in high season.

Restaurants

€€€ over €40   €€ €20-40   € under €20

Price codes refer to the cost of a two-course meal with a drink for one person, including service and cover charge.

For more freedom and independence, especially on a touring holiday with a flexible itinerary, you may need to find and book accommodation yourself. This is not difficult: the internet has made it easy to make reservations in advance.

Hotel pricing in France is normally for the room, not per person. Breakfast is generally not included, but is available for an extra charge of about €12-15 in mid-priced establishments – it is usually cheaper to pop out to a café.

Hotels are graded with a star system, but some hotels fall short of a single star (expect to pay under €40), while others far exceed the requirements for France's maximum grade 'four-star Luxe' (expect to pay over €300 per night). Most have three stars (around €80-140 per double room).

Prices vary considerably by season and from place to place. Prices take a big step up as the summer peak approaches. Expect to see room rates rise sharply at Easter, then in June, and again in July. They step down again at the end of August, making early autumn a good time to visit.

Booking

To visit the most popular parts of the Normandy coast during peak season (July to August), it's wise to plan everything at least two months in advance. Out of high season, though, especially away from the main towns, it is not usually necessary to book more than a day in advance.

Hotels and *chambres d'hôtes* (guest rooms) are easily booked online or by phone. For small, independent, family-run establishments, especially off the beaten track, a smattering of French may be needed. For camping and self-catering, it can be simpler to pre-book a package rather than to arrange independently.

Hotels

In and around Normandy's larger towns, you will find everything from predictable, decent budget hotels to stylish four-star luxe hotels. Almost all towns and many villages have at least one modest, comfortable three-star hotel, generally with its own restaurant. They often have a traditional feel and are sometimes in historic mansions and manor houses (do ask in advance if steep stairs or other access issues may be a problem). If prices are very low, ask carefully about facilities – a bargain-priced hotel room may lack modern amenities.

The major international hotel groups are all present. In addition, the big French chains, all with several hotels in the region, include **Campanile** motels with restaurants, economy motels such as **Formule 1**, which are modern and simple, **Ibis** (functional, budget-priced town hotels), and more upmarket chains **Meridien** and **Sofitel**.

A high proportion of hotels are independent, most of which belong to hotel federations that resemble chains, requiring member establishments to reach a certain standard. Two dependable French hotel and restaurant federations are **Relais & Châteaux**, which offer classic luxury, and **Logis de France**, small, traditional family-run hotels, nearly all with a restaurant.

B&B/chambres d'hôtes
Bed and breakfast accommodation in private homes (usually in a purpose-built extension) is common in rural areas. It provides an inexpensive alternative with the added interest of meeting local people and getting under the surface of Normandy life. These *chambres d'hôtes* (guest rooms) often have nothing more than a simple sign on the front gate. You're welcome to stop and ask for a room. Some provide an evening meal too. All cd'hôtes have to be approved by local authorities.

Gîtes/self-catering
Gîtes – self-catering country cottages – are found all over Normandy in the most rural areas. They're often a bargain, though facilities can be old-fashioned. It is wise to pre-book, either by phone or online (gites-de-france.fr/, in French and English).

For self-catering with all the comforts of home, choose from thousands of modern holiday houses and villas available from a number of UK tour operators and agencies. You can find self-catering in towns, too: *meublés* ('furnished') are vacation apartments. Contact local tourist offices for a list; they can also make bookings.

Campsites
Campsites are the least expensive accommodation and often in the best locations. Most of the larger sites have a number of erected spacious modern tents as well as rows of mobile homes fixed in position. Campsites are carefully regulated and must meet approved standards. They're graded with stars: anything with two or more stars has hot showers and good facilities. Four-star and the even better four-star 'Grand Comfort' sites have excellent amenities, often including a swimming pool. *Camping à la Ferme*, campsites on farms, are a category on their own that tends to be more basic. At the other extreme, Castels et Camping, mainly in superb locations, is a federation of top-quality camps.

Food and drink on the Normandy Coast

Gastronomic region
French tourists happily make their way to Normandy for the pleasures of the table. Normandy's traditional cooking has a highly distinctive regional style, with a strong emphasis on its rich dairy produce, shellfish and good-quality meats, as well as the abundant harvest of its cherry, pear and especially apple orchards.

There are numerous Normandy specialities. The result of all those orchards and dairy farms and picturesque fishing harbours is meals with plenty of local cheeses, butter, and thick, farm-made, semi-sour crème fraîche for savoury cream sauces. Apples may turn up in any course as apple sauces and apple pastry, dry cider and fiery Calvados, and the sherry-like aperitif, *pommeau*.

More than that, Normandy is renowned in France for the sheer size of meals. Normans are trenchermen *par excellence*, spending longer at the table than anyone else in the country. From this arose the tradition of the *trou normand* – literally the 'Norman gap',

Dining tips

Choose a prix-fixe menu
At most restaurants you'll be offered à la carte (list of dishes, individually priced) and a choice of about three menus, that is, *prix fixe* (fixed price) set meals. Typical menu prices might be €20-40. The price difference reflects not differences in quality but in number of courses and difficulty of preparation. In general, to get the best out of a restaurant, and the best value for money, order one of the menus, not à la carte.

Formula for a cheap lunch
For a quick light meal, many restaurants and bars offer an inexpensive fixed-price *formule* without specifying the dishes. It's often a starter and simple main course, or main course and dessert, with a quarter-litre of house wine and a coffee.

What's on the bill?
French restaurant prices always include service and all taxes. It's not necessary to give any extra tip. *Vin compris* means wine included (usually a quarter of a litre of house wine per person); *boisson comprise* means you may have a beer or soft drink instead.

Eat at the right time
Away from resorts and big cities, it can be difficult to find something to eat outside normal mealtimes. Lunch is served generally 1200-1400 (Sunday lunch lasts until 1500), and dinner 1900-2200.

Out of hours dining
Brasseries (breweries) are bars that serve food at any time of day. A *salon de thé* is a smarter alternative for between-meals pastries and other light snacks with tea or coffee.

No need to dress for dinner
Smart casual is the norm in even the best places, though you may dress up if you prefer.

but the custom itself is more elegant than the phrase: a short break between two main courses, in which a tot of Calvados is sipped, supposedly to aid digestion. Nowadays it is more likely to be a Calvados sorbet.

Dairy produce
Some of the best-known French cheeses come from Normandy. Creamy and pungent 'washed-rind' boxed cheeses, made from the milk of grass-fed cows, carry the names of the towns and villages where they were first produced. Among them are Camembert, Pont l'Évêque, Livarot and Pavé d'Auge, all in the Pays d'Auge, and from the other side of the Seine, Neufchâtel (which is usually made in a cute heart shape). Local farm-made crème fraîche is a staple of Normandy's all-important sauces: a rich, smooth, slightly soured thick cream. Normandy butter, processed and wrapped at Isigny, is also counted among the very best and is widely exported all over France and abroad.

Seafood
Expect to find lobsters and crayfish, crabs and spider crabs, oysters, scallops and mussels on almost every menu. They are jointly known as *fruits de mer* and often served in large heaps. Such seafood is another essential ingredient of Normandy's sauces and stews. The main area for shellfish is the Cotentin Peninsula, especially around the scenic ports of Granville and St Vaast-la-Hougue. Fresh fish are also abundant.

Local specialities
Almost every good meal in Normandy includes lashings of cream and a good splash of Calvados or cider. Among the most famous of all Normandy's plethora of local specialities is *tripes à la mode de Caen*, a long-cooked stew of tripe, pig's trotters, vegetables, herbs and Calvados. Another is *Marmite Dieppoise*, a creamy fish-and-shellfish stew supposedly invented at the restaurant from which it takes its name. More generally, *dieppoise*, as in the classic *sole à la dieppoise*, means served in a creamy sauce made with white wine, mussels and crayfish. Other local favourites include charcuterie, especially *andouilles and andouillettes* (chitterling sausages large and small) from the farms of south-western Calvados, and *boudin* (black pudding) from southern Normandy. *Agneau de pré-salé* is the distinctive-tasting tender lamb from the flood meadows around Mont St Michel Bay. While you're at Le Mont-St-Michel, another local treat is *omelette Mère Poulard*, a thick fluffy soufflé omelette.

For something simple, crêpes have long been Normandy's preferred cheap snack. These paper-thin pancakes can be sprinkled with almost anything, sweet or savoury, and are especially popular on the Cotentin Peninsula. To finish the meal, apples, pears and cherries are served in tasty flans and tarts.

Festivals on the Normandy Coast

Normandy's calendar reflects the two great preoccupations of the duchy and its people – good food and the sea. From spring to autumn, food fairs celebrate local produce, and traditional blessings are made for the sea and those who work on it. There are also prestigious arts and music festivals.

February
Granville Carnival 5-day carnival celebrations in Granville starting the Fri before Mardi Gras (carnavaldegranville.fr).

March and April
Festival de Pâques Deauville kicks off the Easter holiday season with 2 weeks of classical music (deauville.org).
La Foire de Pâques A huge annual Easter funfair at Caen, with more than 130 rides, free to enter and lasting 3 weeks.

May and June
Jazz Sous les Pommiers (May) This important week-long annual 'jazz under the apple trees' festival in Coutances draws big crowds to the medieval country town (jazzsouslespommiers.com).
Bénédiction de la Mer (May, on Ascension Day) A devout traditional procession in Etretat to a seashore Mass and a cliff-top blessing.
Pentecôte (May or Jun) The religious holiday of Pentecost (or Whitsun) is a holiday weekend in France.
Yacht rally (Pentecost) Thousands of yachts sail in waters around Cherbourg and the Cotentin.
Fête des Marins et des Pêcheurs (Pentecost) This festival of sailors and fishermen takes the form of a pilgrimage to cliff-top Eglise Notre Dame de Grâce in Honfleur to bless the sea and the sailors (ot-honfleur.fr)

D-Day Commemorations (6 Jun) Veterans and visitors remember and celebrate the hard-won victories on the Landing Beaches, where the towns are decked with Allied and French flags. Bayeux has a D-Day Festival (bayeux-bessin-tourisme.com).

July
Fêtes Médiévales (1st weekend) A jolly celebration of the Middle Ages in the medieval streets of Bayeux with parades in medieval dress, singing, dancing celebrating the end of the Hundred Years' War (mairie-bayeux.fr).
Fête de la Mer et du Maquereau Weekend sea festival in Trouville-sur-Mer with mackerel tasting and a festive procession and blessing of boats (trouvillesurmer.org).

August
Grand Pardon (Sun nearest end of Jul; can be in Jul or Aug) Atmospheric traditional events in Granville, with banners, torchlight parade, outdoor Mass and blessings of the sea and of the boats (ville-granville.fr/grand_pardon.asp).

September
Festival du Cinéma Américain (10 days at start of Sep) Stars, glamour and screenings in Deauville of the year's best releases from Hollywood and American independents (festival-deauville.com).

October
Festival des Coquillages et Crustacés (usually 1st weekend) The leading shellfish port of Granville celebrates and shares its speciality (normandie-tourisme.fr).

November
Foire aux Harengs or Fête du Hareng (mid-Nov) Herrings are celebrated at this quayside festival in Dieppe, and at most other towns on the Alabaster Coast (dieppetourisme.com).

Shopping on the Normandy Coast

Most shopping areas have excellent *perfumiers*. Other shops sell an extensive choice of attractive and affordable good-quality kitchenware, household goods and wine paraphernalia. Le Havre and Caen have pedestrianized shopping areas packed with good shops. Some department store chains are renowned for glamour and style, especially Galeries Lafayettes, which has a branch in Caen.

Arts and crafts
Traditional crafts and trades survive in several parts of Normandy. Knitted goods (*tricoterie*) are a tradition of the fishing ports, many of which now have fine knitwear boutiques. In the old metalworking and market town of Villedieu-les-Poêles (30 km inland from Granville), gleaming copper pots and pans still hang outside shops in the main street just as they have for centuries. Look out for antiques too, in street markets, *brocantes* (second-hand shops) and *antiquaires* (antiques dealers). You may find even discover good pieces of Normandy's classic 18th- and 19th-century local blue and white patterned faïence and porcelain known as faïence de Rouen or, in English, "Rouen ware".

Clothes
Stylish fashion boutiques and small independent stores give character to the shopping streets of all Normandy's main towns. Even smaller towns keep up to date with latest

French fashions. Look especially for beautiful shoes, jewellery, handbags and lingerie. Menswear shops no less than womenswear have originality and flair. There are delightful children's clothes too. Even babies are well dressed in France.

Farm produce

All over Normandy, away from the big towns and resorts, quiet country roads pass farm gates with signs inviting you to a *dégustation* (tasting). They are seen especially in the Pays d'Auge, behind the Côte Fleurie. On offer are cider, *calvados* and other alcoholic apple drinks, and pear drinks too, as well as fresh fruit juices, cheeses, farmhouse pâtés and preserved meats, and honey from their own hives. Tastings are usually free, and there may even be a free tour too, showing how the produce is made. Although there is no obligation, etiquette requires that having tasted, you will buy – at least a small amount. Prices are usually a little less than in a supermarket. Generally, the goods are suitable for taking home, although strong cheeses should not be kept in the car too long!

Food and drink

In any Normandy town you'll find busy specialist stores selling locally produced food and drink. The *traiteur* and *charcuterie* both have *boudins*, *andouillettes* and other prepared and preserved meats and ready-to-eat cooked dishes and salads. *Boucherie* is a butcher's shop. An *epicerie* stocks everyday foods, including calvados and cider, while the classier *epicerie fine* caters to gourmet tastes, and generally has a top-quality cheese counter, perhaps *crème fraîche* ladled from a tub and fresh butter cut from a large slab. *Boulangerie* is a baker's, often selling country-style breads as well as traditional baguette and *flute*. They may sell pastries too, but a better place for those is the *pâtisserie*, the pastry-cook's. *Chocolatiers* and *confiseurs* (or *confiserie*) make and sell confectionery, while a *glacier* (it sounds cold!) specialises in ice-cream. A *supermarché* is a small self-service shop, while an edge-of-town *hypermarché* – a large supermarket – will stock a full range of goods from around the world.

Markets

Most towns in Normandy have at least one farmer's market (*marché*) per week, either in a centuries-old market square or a covered *halles*. Among the best of Normandy's street markets are in Caen and Dieppe. The bigger markets include dozens of stalls selling inexpensive clothes, kitchenware, household items and other goods. Freshly gathered fruit and vegetables in season are piled high. Look out for stalls with local Normandy cheeses, creamy white heart shapes of Neufchâtel or squares of Livarot and Pont l'Evêque and circles of Camembert, as well as ready-to-eat stews and whole roasted free-range chickens off the spit, a multitude of dried sausages, jars of preserved meats and bottles of local cider and other drinks. Markets are usually held in the morning only, from about 0700 to 1300.

Seafood

At fishing ports, the fresh catch is laid out and sold each morning from stalls on the quayside. Sole, brill and mackerel are plentiful. Early in the day, you can see it being carted straight into the kitchens of waterfront restaurants. Queues of discerning locals form to buy the best of fish and shellfish, usually by the half-kilo, the kilo or even larger amounts, such as 5 kg of the popular Coquilles St Jacques (scallops) for about €20. Remember to keep live shellfish cold, but not on ice, and not in an airtight bag. Eat them within a day or two.

Essentials A-Z

Children
Normandy, like most regions of France, is extremely family friendly. Children are welcomed in restaurants with their own menu. Hotels often have family rooms, or can wheel in an extra cot or bed for a few euros extra. Discounts are usually offered at sights and attractions.

Customs and immigration
UK and other EU citizens do not need a visa to visit France. Travellers from USA, Australia, New Zealand and Canada may stay up to 90 days without a visa. There are no restrictions on importing legal articles for personal use.

Disabled travellers
France is aware of the needs of disabled travellers but provision for them is patchy. New public buildings are obliged to provide access and facilities, but problems can be acute in areas with cobbled paving and medieval buildings. For parking, display your EU blue photocard as in the UK. French organizations for the disabled focus on residents, not tourists. Normandy Tourism produces useful booklets (in French, but using easy-to-understand symbols) detailing tourist establishments with facilities for the disabled. They are available online at normandie-tourisme. fr/normandy-tourism/more-information/ disabled-friendly-normandy-179-2.html.

Electricity
The power is supply in France is 220 volts. Circular 2-pin plugs are used.

Etiquette
Most French people rigorously observe conventions of politeness, always shaking hands on first introduction, moving on to kisses on the cheek (2, 3 or 4 depending on the nature of the relationship) with friends. The formal word *vous* should be used for 'you' until a fine line of intimacy has been crossed, then you should stick to *tu*. Punctuality is fairly strictly observed. Dress in public places is usually smart casual and stylish. Address strangers as *Monsieur*, *Madame* or *Mademoiselle*. Entering or leaving small shops or offices, especially in rural areas, greet those inside with a quick '*Messieurs-dames*'.

Health
Comprehensive travel and medical insurance is recommended. EU citizens should apply for a free European Health Insurance Card or EHIC (ehic.org), which entitles you to emergency medical treatment on the same terms as French nationals. Note that you will have to pay all charges and prescriptions up front and be reimbursed once you return home. If you develop a minor ailment while on holiday a visit to any pharmacy will allow you to discuss your concerns with highly qualified staff, who can give medical advice and recommend treatment. Outside normal opening hours, the address of the nearest duty pharmacy (*pharmacie de garde*) is displayed in the pharmacy window. The out-of-hours number for a local doctor (*médecin généraliste*) may also be listed.

In a serious emergency, go to the accident and emergency department (*urgences*) at the nearest Centre Hospitalier (numbers listed at the end of each chapter) or call an ambulance (SAMU) by dialling 15.

Insurance
Comprehensive travel and medical insurance is strongly recommended, as the European Health Insurance Card (EHIC) does not cover medical repatriation, ongoing medical treatment or treatment considered to be non-urgent. Check for exclusions if you mean to engage in risky sports. Keep

all insurance documents to hand; a good way to keep track of your policies is to email the details to yourself. Make sure you have adequate insurance when hiring a car and always ask how much excess you are liable for if the vehicle is returned with any damage. It is generally worth paying a little more for collision damage waiver. If driving your own vehicle to France, contact your insurers before you travel to ensure you are adequately covered, and keep the documents in your vehicle in case you need to prove it.

Money
The currency in France is the euro (€). Euros are available from ATMs using credit or debit cards. Credit cards are widely accepted by shops, restaurants, museums, attractions, petrol stations, etc, but may be refused in shops for purchases below about €5. Remember you need your PIN for every transaction. Cash is needed for buses, taxis, bars and markets.

Opening hours
Few shops open on Sun in France and many shops are also closed on Mon. The exception is in popular tourist centres and resorts. Town centre shops are open Tue-Sat 0900-1200 or 1230 and 1400 or 1430-1800. Food shops often open earlier in the morning, and a few (especially *boulangeries* and *pâtisseries*) open on Sun morning. Stores usually open Mon-Sat 0900-1830, but often have 1 or more late evenings in mid-week.

Police
To call police in an emergency, dial 17. French police are divided into different forces with different roles. *Gendarmes* are armed units on call to deal with crime, especially outside urban areas. *Police Nationale* are ordinary employees under the control of the mayor, dealing with routine policing issues. CRS have a wide remit to prevent violent civil disturbance.

Post
The post office (PTT, or La Poste) provides communications services, generally including stamps, phone, and internet access. Offices are open (with local variations) during normal working hours Mon-Fri, and usually Sat morning. Stamps (*timbres*) can also be bought in newsagents and little stores known as *tabacs*. A stamp for an ordinary letter (up to 20 g) or postcard within France costs €0.57; within the EU €0.77; to the US, Canada, Australia and most other countries €0.89. Letter boxes are yellow.

Safety
All towns and rural areas in Normandy are generally safe, with little crime. However, sensible precautions should be taken; for example, don't leave anything valuable on view in cars.

Telephone
French phone numbers indicate which region and which town they are in (all Normandy numbers begin with 02, for example), but there are no area codes and you must dial all 10 digits when phoning from inside France. The prefix for France is +33 and drop the initial 0 of the number you are phoning. For international operator assistance, dial 3212.

France is well covered by mobile phone (cell phone) reception. European (including UK) visitors can use their phones normally. Visitors from the US and Australia should call their provider to check their package. On arrival in France you will receive a text informing you of the charges. All public phones required a pre-paid card, available from newsagents, *tabacs*, etc.

Time
France uses Central European Standard Time and Central European Daylight Saving Time (ie GMT+1 and GMT+2 respectively). CET Daylight Saving Time (Summer Time) starts at 0200 on the last Sun in Mar and ends at 0300 on the last Sun in Oct.

Tipping

Tipping is not necessary in France. Hotel, restaurant and bar bills include service and no tip is expected, although small change is often left for service at an outdoor table. Taxi drivers do not expect tips, though many people do round the fare up. For good service anywhere, just say 'Merci!'.

Tourist information

For regional information, contact the **Normandy Tourism** (CRT Normandie), T02 32 33 79 00, normandie-tourisme.fr. For local information: Caen, T02 31 27 14 14, tourisme.caen.fr; Cherbourg-Octeville, T02 33 93 52 02, cherbourgtourisme.com; Deauville, T02 31 14 40 00, deauville.org; Dieppe, T02 32 14 40 60, dieppetourisme. com; Granville, T02 33 91 30 03, granville-tourisme.fr; Honfleur, T02 31 89 23 30, ot-honfleur.fr; Le Havre T02 32 74 04 04, lehavretourisme.com; Le Mont-St-Michel, T02 33 60 14 30, ot-montsaintmichel.com.

Contents

Footprint features

Caen & the Landing Beaches

Caen

Caen needs time to be thoroughly explored. Fortified by William the Conqueror, this city became his new capital of Normandy. The former capital of Rouen was, he felt, too vulnerable to attack from the Franks. The mighty rampart of his château is still the centre of the city, while the main shopping streets, the Vaugeux restaurant district and Quai Vendeuvre leisure area are all at its foot, extending away from the south side of the castle walls. Several of Caen's other principal sights ring the edges of the city centre. Each one of them deserves unhurried attention, and you should allow plenty of time too for the journey from one to the other. The church of the Abbaye aux Hommes, for example, the Men's Abbey where William the Conqueror's tomb lies in front of the altar, stands at a very proper distance from the Abbaye aux Dames! Both are unmissable works of Norman architecture, built as part of the penance undertaken by William and his wife Mathilde for their incestuous marriage. For a moment's quiet repose, the lovely Jardin des Plantes lies north of the central district. It's on the way to Le Mémorial, a museum complex on the northern ring road dedicated to honouring those who died in the Second World War, providing a record of the conflict and explaining its background.

Arriving in Caen

Getting there
The bus station is at Place de la Gare (no telephone enquiries). See page 12 for regional bus travel. The train station is also at Place de la Gare, T02 31 83 70 47. See page 11 for regional rail travel.

Getting around
A fast modern city transport system of 33 bus routes and two tram lines is operated by **Twisto** ① *T02 31 15 55 55, twisto.fr*. Maps at the stops show which bus or tram you need to reach other parts of the city or to reach the sights. A single ticket costs €1.30, while a pass for 10 journeys costs €11.30. The 24-hour pass is a bargain at just €3.65. Twisto offer several other fare discount options, including a return trip to a cinema for €5.60 – which includes seeing a film! Tickets can be bought on the bus, or using ticket machines at the stops, from 40 shops and bars around town (displaying a sign, Point de Vente Twisto), at the bus station, or from the **Espace Transport Twisto boutique** ① *15 rue de Geôle, T02 31 15 55 55, Mon-Fri 0800-1830, Sat 1000-1230, 1330-1700*.

If you're staying a while, sign up for **V'eol** ① *T0800 20 03 06, veol.caen.fr*, the town's bicycle-hire scheme. Once you have an account, a bike can be picked up (using your credit card) at stands all over town. The first 30 minutes are free; second, third and fourth 30-minute periods cost €1 each. Thereafter, it's €2 for each 30 minutes.

Tourist information
Office de Tourisme ① *12 place St Pierre, T02 31 27 14 14, tourisme.caen.fr. Mar Mon-Sat 0930-1300, 1400-1830; Apr-Jun and Sep Mon-Sat 0930-1830, Sun 1000-1300; Jul-Aug Mon-Sat 0900-1900, Sun 1000-1300, 1400-1700; Oct-Feb Mon Sat 0930 1300 and 1400-1800*. Available at the tourist office, Le Pass Tourisme is a little book of vouchers giving valuable discounts at numerous sights, attractions, shops and restaurants. The price? It's absolutely free.

Places in Caen → *For listings, see pages 30-34.*

Le Château de Caen
① *Main entrance is accessed from rue Poissonnerie, in front of Eglise St-Pierre, chateau-caen.eu. Free access.*
Climb the grass-covered slope and cross a dry moat to enter William the Conqueror's castle walls, which still dominate the city centre. A drawbridge and fortified gateway allow entry through Porte St-Pierre (opposite Eglise St-Pierre in the city centre) or the massive Porte des Champs (on the east side) into the heavily defended enclosure. The surprise inside is how little remains of the ducal buildings. The destruction of the original castle keep began at the Revolution and continued until the 19th century. There was further damage during the war. Instead the ramparts enclose a vast space broken up by a few small structures. The partly rebuilt, mainly 15th-century Eglise St-Georges once served the 'parish' living and working within the castle walls. The 17th-century Governor's Lodge, built against the southern ramparts, now houses the Musée de Normandie. The low, partly underground Musée des Beaux Arts was built against the eastern ramparts in the 1960s. Over on the west side, beside the ruins of the keep, stands one impressive remnant of the ducal period, the 12th-century Salle de l'Echiquier (Exchequer Room). Despite the name (which was

given in the 19th century), this was the dukes' two-storey Great Hall, with kitchens on the ground floor and lavish banqueting chamber above.

Musée des Beaux Arts (Caen Fine Arts Museum)
ⓘ *Le Château, T02 31 30 47 70, mba.caen.fr. Wed-Mon 0930-1800. To see permanent collection €3.10, concessions €2.10. Additional €2 (concessions €1) to see a temporary exhibition.*

In an unobtrusive modern building of Caen stone just inside the Château entrance is the Fine Arts Museum. In a series of rooms, a wide range of artworks focuses mainly on 16th- to 17th-century French, Italian and Flemish painting, including pieces by Tintoretto, Breughel the Younger, Rembrandt and a good collection by minor figures. Among earlier periods, one of the museum's greatest possessions is Rogier van der Weyden's *Virgin and Child*. In downstairs rooms devoted to modern art there are numerous pictures depicting Normandy scenes and landscapes, including lesser works by some of the greatest names, among them Dufy, Monet, Boudin, Bonnard, Vuillard, Corot and Courbet. Paintings showing pre-war Caen are especially interesting. The museum also hosts temporary exhibitions.

Musée de Normandie (Normandy Museum)
ⓘ *Le Château, T02 31 30 47 60, musee-de-normandie.eu. Daily 0930-1800 (closed Tue Nov-May). €3.10-7.10 (concessions €2.10-5.10), depending on what is currently on show.*

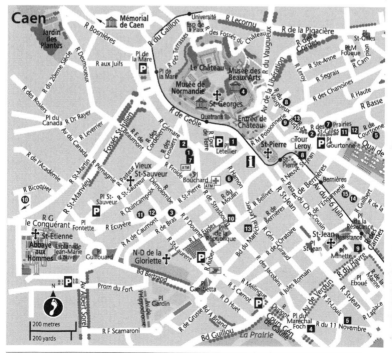

Interesting diverse collections all about Normandy include geology, archaeology, farming, history, folk culture, and how the region's traditional arts and crafts gave rise to its modern industries. There are also summer-long temporary exhibitions.

Eglise St-Pierre
ⓘ *Place St-Pierre, T02 31 27 14 14. Daily 0900-1800.*

Standing close to the main south entrance of the Château, St-Pierre is the highly decorated parish church of Caen city centre, a remarkable survivor of the wartime assault. Its rebuilt 75-m spire provides an easy-to-spot landmark. The building, constructed over a 300-year period starting in the 13th century, is a fine example of late Gothic, with an apse incorporating rich Renaissance ornamentation. Inside there is good stained glass, notably the rose window on the west front. Notice the amazingly detailed carved allegorical figures on some of the capitals. A display of photographs shows how the church looked immediately after the Allied bombing in 1944. What also makes the church especially interesting is that it is being painstakingly restored to its original condition. The result is newly carved Flamboyant and Renaissance white exterior stonework, giving an impression of how such churches looked when they had just been built.

Where to stay 🛏
Central Hôtel **1**
Dauphin Best Western **2**
Etap Hotel Caen Gare **3**
Hôtel Bristol **5**
Hôtel de France **6**
Hôtel des Quatrans **7**
Hôtel du Château **8**
Hôtel du Havre **9**
Hôtel Kyriad Caen Centre **10**
Hôtel Malherbe **4**
Ibis Caen Centre **11**
Mercure Port de Plaisance **12**
Moderne Best Western **13**

Restaurants, bars & clubs 🍴
ArchiDona **1**
Café Latin **3**
Café Mancel **4**
Incognito **5**
Ivan Vautier (Le Pressoir) **10**
La Maison d'Italie **6**
Le Bistrot **8**
Le Bouchon du Vaugueux **9**
Le Carré **14**
Le Chic **7**
Le French Café **15**
Le Vertigo **11**
Lounge Café **12**
Maître Corbeau **13**
Quai 52 **2**

Abbaye aux Hommes (Men's Abbey)
ⓘ *Esplanade Jean-Marie Louvel, T02 31 30 42 81. caen.fr/abbayeauxhommes. Entry to the Abbey church is free – see Abbatiale-St-Etienne below. Entry to the monastic buildings (town hall) is only on guided tours. Guided tours daily at 0930, 1100, 1430 and 1600, with additional tours in Jul-Aug (in Jan and Dec, no tours on Sat-Sun).*

Although the Men's Abbey was founded by William the Conqueror, most of what can be seen today dates from later centuries. While much survives of the original abbey church (see Abbatiale-St-Etienne below), the monastic buildings themselves date mainly from as recently as the 18th century, when they were entirely rebuilt. Only the grand 14th-century Gothic hall known as the Salle des Gardes predates the reconstruction. The new abbey briefly served its intended purpose in the decades before the Revolution. Since 1965 they have been used as the Hôtel de Ville (town hall), with very attractive formal gardens laid out in front. Parts of the building can be visited on guided tours, which reveal a lovely cloister and exceptionally beautiful and elegant interiors containing the finest craftsmanship, especially in the oak-panelled former refectory.

Abbatiale St-Etienne

ⓘ *Abbaye aux Hommes (Men's Abbey), Esplanade Jean-Marie Louvel. Daily 0815-1200 and 1400-1930. Free.*

Begun in 1067 and supposedly completed by 1081, the abbey's St-Etienne church is considered to be among the great buildings of Europe. Constructed in haste because William the Conqueror wished to be buried in the church (which in fact he was just six years after it was 'completed'), much more work remained to be done, and continued for some 200 years. The curious blend of 11th-century Norman Romanesque in its purest form with 12th- and then 13th-century Norman Gothic construction is unexpectedly harmonious and serene. There is a sense of great size, with little adornment yet delicate proportions. In front of the altar lies a marble slab to mark William's tomb. The original tomb was destroyed in the Wars of Religion, and even the replacement was destroyed, in the Revolution. It is said that just a single thigh bone of the Conqueror remains buried in his grave.

Abbaye aux Dames (Women's Abbey)

ⓘ *Place Reine Mathilde, T02 31 06 98 98. Church daily about 0900-1800, may be closed 1200-1400. Free. Former convent guided visits daily 1430 and 1600. Free.*

The penance required of William and Mathilde by the Pope for their incestuous union (they were cousins) was to found four hospitals and two abbeys. William decided that all should be in Caen. His Abbaye aux Hommes was matched by Mathilde's Abbaye aux Dames a mile away. Both were rebuilt in the 18th century, neither is still an abbey, but at both the church is an impressive survivor from the time of the Dukes. Now housing the Basse-Normandie Conseil Régional (Regional Council), the Women's Abbey suffered from some unsuccessful 18th- and 19th-century restorations. However, Mathilde's simple church in creamy stone, the Eglise Abbatiale de la Trinité – much smaller than William's – remains a fine example of Norman Romanesque architecture, incorporating 12th- and 13th-century early Gothic developments. Inside, Mathilde lies beneath a slab of dark marble in the chancel. Narrow steps lead down to an atmospheric crypt packed with pillars. The neighbouring former convent buildings (guided tours only) include delightful three-sided cloisters, an oval lavatorium (washroom) and a spacious Hall with a twin staircase.

Le Mémorial de Caen

ⓘ *Esplanade Général Eisenhower, T02 31 06 06 45, memorial-caen.fr. Mar-Dec daily 0900-1900 (Tue-Sun 0930-1800 during approximate period 12 Nov-5 Feb). Ticket desk closes 1 hr 15 mins before museum. €18.50; €15 concessions; free for under 10s, war veterans and unemployed. Many more concessions available, see website. Family pass €45 (for 2 adults and at least 1 child 10-18 years).Temporary exhibitions may have a separate entry charge, or may be free.*

A sombre memorial to those who died as a result of the Second World War, Le Mémorial is also a museum about the development of modern warfare in relation to the social and political background, progress and eventual conclusion of that war. A large section is devoted to the French experience, and another to the experience of the world as a whole. In addition, it has taken on a broader mission to oppose war and conflict. To some extent, the task is too vast, with the result that some aspects of the Second World War are dealt with too sketchily. Others are examined with impressive thoroughness.

Descend the spiral staircase at the start of the exhibition which leads down, step by ominous step, past posters and photographs and news media of the period marking all the significant dates, from 9 November 1918 down into the growth of Nazism in Germany,

Caen bombing

Caen was a prime objective for the Allied forces making their way inland from the Landing Beaches. However, Panzer tank divisions effectively protected the city. To wrest Caen from German hands, on 7 July 1944 Allied planes dropped 2500 tons of bombs on the city. Fighting for control of Caen continued until 22 August, by which time 75% of its buildings had been destroyed and thousands of its citizens killed.

the acquiescence of other nations, and the eventual world war. There the exhibition expands to track the political, military and social course of the war, with a vast amount of authentic historical material, including such items as Nazi flags, the outfit worn by inmates of death camps, military maps and genuine weaponry. Important letters on display include one from Albert Einstein to President Roosevelt suggesting that nuclear fusion could form the basis of a bomb. There are also wartime letters from soldiers – including Germans – to their families. Films using newsreel of the period are devoted to key periods in the war, including a poignant and fascinating account of the Battle of Britain.

Caen listings

For hotel and restaurant price codes and other relevant information, see pages 13-17.

Where to stay

Caen *p24, map p26*

€€€ Hôtel Dauphin, rue Gémare, T02 31 86 22 26, le-dauphin-normandie.com. This comfortable, pleasant **Best Western** hotel in a converted former priory near the Château, close to the pedestrianized shopping streets, is a contender for the best place in town. Moderately sized, well-equipped rooms, attractively decorated in pale colours and modern style, but with genuine old beams. Useful free parking in the hotel's (cramped and hard to use) car park. There's also a restaurant.

€€€ Hôtel Malherbe, place Maréchal Foch, T02 31 27 57 57, caen-hotel-centre.com. This **Best Western Plushotel** may suit some as it is a little off the usual tourist beat, beside Caen's racecourse, several mins' walk from the city centre and main sights. Occupying a large corner building fronting on to a square with a war memorial, it has a classic, traditional feel. Bedrooms are varied, mainly with muted chocolatey tones, adequately large, clean and comfortable. Free Wi-Fi. Private parking.

€€€ Hôtel Moderne, bd Maréchal Leclerc, T02 31 86 04 23, hotel-caen.com. Looking on to a square close to pedestrianized shopping streets and a few mins' walk from the main sights, this comfortable city centre 3-star **Best Western** hotel has reasonably spacious, if rather dated rooms in smart, sober colours with polished wooden furnishings. There's also useful private parking.

€€€-€€ Hôtel Mercure Port de Plaisance, rue de Courtonne, T02 31 47 24 24, mercure.com. A bright modern low-rise close to place de Courtonne in the heart of Caen, and looking on to the Port de Plaisance, this reliable, well-run chain hotel offers among the best of 3-star comfort and amenities.

Public areas are spacious and plush. Varied bedrooms have simple, calm colour schemes.

€€ Hôtel Bristol, rue du 11 Novembre, T02 31 84 59 76, hotelbristolcaen.com. North of the River Orne, but close to the railway station (and the racetrack, if that's of interest), this modestly priced family-run hotel has small, simple but attractive rooms in pale tones, with fabrics in warm colours. There's a homely bar/salon, free Wi-Fi, and a decent buffet breakfast is served.

€€ Hôtel de France, rue de la Gare, T02 31 52 16 99. South of the River Orne, this 2-star is on a bleak main road close to the railway station. Well-kept rooms in pastel colours have wooden furnishings, are double glazed, adequately equipped and popular with business travellers. Tram and bus routes outside provide a quick link to the centre.

€€ Hôtel des Quatrans, rue Gémare, T02 31 86 25 57, hotel-des-quatrans.com. An efficient modern city centre hotel with well-kept, small and simple but comfortable rooms in rich, dark tones. The hotel stands on the edge of the pedestrianized shopping area close to the Château. Free Wi-Fi is available. Downstairs is the hotel's excellent **ArchiDona** restaurant (see page 31).

€€ Hôtel du Château, av du 6 Juin, T02 31 86 15 37, hotel-chateau-caen.com. It's on a busy street just a few moments from the Château and the Port de Plaisance, and beside the tramline, yet this basic and inexpensive 2-star is quiet and comfortable. It's 6 storeys high (there's a lift), with bright and colourful decor, Wi-Fi access and its own pay-to-use car park.

€€ Hôtel du Havre, rue du Havre, T02 31 86 19 80, hotelduhavre.com. Straightforward and functional, decorated in warm colours, this simple but adequate city centre backstreet accommodation in an unpretentious modern building is excellent value for money and is not without homely charm. Wi-Fi is included.

€€ Hôtel Kyriad Caen Centre, 1 place de la République, T02 31 86 55 33, hotel-caen-centre.com. Rooms are small and simple, but modern and decent, at this city centre low-budget chain hotel. There are a few pleasant little extras, such as free Wi-Fi, and free coffee and biscuits in every room.

€€-€ **Ibis Caen Centre**, place Courtonne, T02 31 95 88 88, ibishotel.com. A branch of the familiar Ibis chain is well located in the heart of Caen close to the Château and the Port de Plaisance. Rooms are plain and simple, highly functional and admittedly charmless, but adequately equipped and affordable. The hotel has its own restaurant, and a bar open day and night.

€ **Central Hôtel**, place Jean Letellier, T02 31 86 18 52, centralhotel-caen.com. Some of the lowest prices in town are charged for these traditional, and perhaps rather dated, simple bedrooms in a basic building with few facilities. The location is its best feature – near the Château and main shopping streets.

€ **Etap/Ibis Hôtel Caen Gare**, 16 place de la Gare, T08 92 68 09 05, www.accor.com This Etap – due to become an Ibis – is south of the River Orne, right next to Caen railway station. For those unfamiliar with Etap's budget formula, every room is identical, modern and tiny, with blue and white decor. Facilities are cleverly functional yet adequate, and prices could hardly be lower. Buffet breakfast is available.

⑦ Restaurants

Caen *p24, map p26*

€€ **Café Mancel**, Musée des Beaux Arts, Le Château, T02 31 86 63 64, cafemancel. com. Tue-Sat lunch and dinner, Sun lunch. A useful place for a drink or snack (including such satisfying things as bread and cheese) or a full meal of classic French dishes when you're visiting the Château, this smart, contemporary café at the Fine Arts Museum is worth returning to for live music evenings across the range from jazz to classical.

€€ **Incognito**, rue de Courtonne, T02 31 28 36 60, stephanecarbone.fr. 1230-14, 1930-2200 (closed Sat midday,

and Sun). One of Caen's most highly rated restaurants, right in the city centre, Michelin-starred **Incognito** has contemporary decor in warm colours, with views into the kitchen. Refined imaginative dishes are elegantly presented (including a menu devoted to lobster), but prices are high.

€€ **Ivan Vautier**, av Henri Chéron, T02 31 73 32 71, ivanvautier.com. 1215-1315, 1915-2115 (closed Sun dinner, and Mon). Just off the ring road on the southwest side of town, this Michelin-starred restaurant in a former coaching inn is indeed worth the journey. Well known to locals (often by its former name, Le Pressoir), this is a chic, contemporary setting for French regional variations on Normandy cuisine, using the best seasonal ingredients. It's also a stylishly modern 4-star hotel.

€€ **Le Bouchon du Vaugueux**, rue Graindorge, T02 31 44 26 26, bouchondu vaugueux.com.Tue-Sat 1200-1400 and 1900-2200, usually closed Aug. On the corner of an 'old quarter' backstreet, this unpretentious spot is one of the best value little eating places in town. Following the tradition of a typical *bouchon* in Lyon (where the word means a good, simple bistro specializing in local dishes), there's a menu of the day with seasonal local fare at a very modest price. It's small, so reservation is advisable.

€€-€ **ArchiDona**, rue Gémare, T02 31 85 30 30, archidona.fr. Tue-Sat 1200-1400, 1900-2130 (2200 Fri-Sat). A lively and popular yet refined, rather smart eating place near the Château, the ArchiDona has a thoroughly modern ambience, pale wicker and white decor and ever-changing menus of tasty and original Mediterranean-oriented cuisine. Excellent value menu for early diners.

€€-€ **La Maison d'Italie**, 10 rue Hamon, T02 31 86 38 02, lamaisonditalie.fr. Sat 1200-1530, 1800-2330; Mon-Fri and Sun 1200-1500, 1800-2300. Bright, brisk and popular child-friendly eatery serving up pizzas, pasta and other Italian classics. Nothing Norman in sight, but good-value dining in a pedestrian street near the Château.

€€-€ **Maître Corbeau**, rue Buquet, T02 31 93 93 00, caen.maitre-corbeau.com. Tue-Fri 1145-1330, Mon-Sat 1900-2230. Closed for about 2 weeks in winter and 3 weeks in summer. Cheese mad and decorated with a chaotic assortment of knick-knacks, cheese boxes, labels and anything cow related, this fun little restaurant proudly offers La Cuisine au Fromage. No surprise, then, that the emphasis is firmly on dairy produce, with meat in cheese sauces, cheese salads and a big choice of cheese fondues. Enjoy a chocolate fondue for dessert.

€ **Le Bistrot**, 12 rue du Vaugueux, T02 31 93 20 30. Lunch and dinner daily. With so many hungry tourists wandering up and down the delightful traffic-free streets in Caen's tiny 'old quarter' – a fragment near the Château that remained unscathed after the destruction in 1944 – it's wise to choose carefully. With its blue-painted exterior timbers, comfortable pub-like interior and tempting outdoor terrace tables, this place is popular with locals and stands out for traditional brasserie-style cooking at an affordable price.

€ **Quai 52**, rue des Prairies St-Gilles, T02 31 44 18 06. Mon-Sat 1200-1400, 1900-2230. On a centrally located site which previously changed hands frequently, **Quai 52**, describing itself as a 'Brasserie Plus', has made a success with its formula of good, inexpensive brasserie fare, all (except the ice cream) freshly made on the premises. A speciality is North African roast lamb. Sit indoors or at tables on the pavement.

Cafés

Café Latin, 135 rue St-Pierre, T02 31 85 26 36. Mon-Sat 0830-0100. Always busy, from morning coffee to late-night drinks. The gaudy exterior draws you into this Spanish-oriented café and bar with atmospheric bare stone and wooden beams. Simple inexpensive meals are available; for example, Spanish omelette and fries.

Lounge Café, 2 place Malherbe, T02 31 36 04 04. Mon-Wed 1200-1400, Thu-Sat 1200-

1500, 1900-2200, Sun 1200-1500. A small, relaxed place with cool young style inside, and tables outside on the attractive little square where rue St-Pierre meets rue Ecuyère. Popular with students.

🌓 Bars and clubs

Caen p24, map p26
Le Carré, 32 quai Vendeuvre, T02 31 38 90 90. Tue-Sun from 2230. Smart dress and over 27s only (20 on Wed and Thu) allowed at this crowded rock and retro club by the Port de Plaisance. Lots of theme nights and a focus on 70s/80s music. Le French Café is upstairs.

Le Chic, 19 rue des Prairies St-Gilles, place Courtonne, T02 31 94 48 72, lechic.fr. Tue-Sat from 2330. Upbeat crowded disco with a 1980s feel and very varied music with the emphasis on dance rhythms. Caribbean nights Tue and Thu. In the city centre close to the waterside.

Le French Café, 32 quai Vendeuvre, T02 31 50 10 02. Tue-Sun 1800-0300. Tue: singles. Wed: rock. A good place to start your evening, or finish it, this relaxed, fun cocktail bar is on the theme of a café in Provence, complete with a plane tree and even a little second-hand shop. Almost all the music is French.

Le Vertigo, 14 rue Ecuyère, T02 31 85 43 12. Mon-Sat 1000-0100. Tiny, packed and trendy, with wooden benches and stone walls, relaxed atmosphere, rock music, their own jug cocktails and amiable service.

🎭 Entertainment

Caen p24, map p26
Children

Festyland, Route de Caumont, Bretteville-sur-Odon, T02 31 75 04 04, festyland.com. Good old-fashioned family fun is on offer at the leisure park on the southwestern edge of the city. It's themed around a fanciful version of Normandy's history, with simple rides and entertainments based on Vikings, William the Conqueror, pirates and the Middle Ages. There's a picnic area and 4 family-friendly restaurants, too.

Music and theatre

Comédie de Caen, 1 square du Théâtre, Hérouville St-Clair and 32 rue des Cordes, Caen, T02 31 46 27 29, comediedecaen.com. Daytime and evening performances are staged throughout the year. Tickets typically cost about €20-24, €14-20 concessions, €8 children 11 and over, €4 children 4-11. The Comédie de Caen is a major host for cultural events in Normandy. Located in 2 theatres, it stages a wide variety of traditional and modern works across the range from dance to concerts to circus. Its main venue is the 700-seat Théâtre d'Hérouville, in Herouville, a suburban 'new town' on the city's northeast. The 2nd venue is the 300-seat **Théâtre des Cordes**, at 32 rue des Cordes, in Caen city centre.
Le Cargo, 9 cours Caffarelli, T02 31 86 79 31, lecargo.fr. Ticket office open Tue-Sat 1400-1900. Tickets typically €15-30. You can catch up with a whole spectrum of live new bands and latest sounds at this concert venue and packed dance club, located across the water where the Port de Plaisance meets the River Orne.
Orchestre de Caen, Auditorium Jean-Pierre Dautel (formerly Grand Auditorium de Caen), 1 rue du Carel, T02 31 30 46 86 (for tickets), caenlamer.fr/orchestre_de_caen. Ticket desk Mon-Fri 1000-1800, Sat 1000-1230, closed during school holidays. Tickets typically cost around €15-20. Resident orchestra performing a wide variety of high-quality concerts from baroque to contemporary classical composers, as well as choral music and even jazz.
Théâtre de Caen, 135 bd du Maréchal Leclerc, T02 31 30 48 00, theatre.caen.fr. Tickets from €5 to €55, with a variety of reductions and concessions depending on the performances. There are no performances in Jul and Aug. The 1000-seat auditorium of Caen's city centre theatre is the venue for an extensive programme of high-quality modern and classical music, opera, dance, plays and arts performances. In addition there are other stage entertainments like acrobats and comedians, and in summer, when the theatre is closed, free events in the square outside.
Zénith, 6 rue Joseph Philippon, T02 31 29 14 38, zenith-caen.fr. Caen's 7000-seat auditorium hosts major stage performances by local, French and international names. There are shows in all genres, from ballet to world music, but the emphasis is on rock and pop.

🛒 Shopping

Caen p24, map p26
Clothing
Galeries Lafayette, 108 bd Maréchal Leclerc, T02 31 39 31 00, galerieslafayette. com/magasin-caen. Mon-Sat 0930-1930. Browse latest French style and quality at this upmarket fashion and furnishings department store in the heart of the city centre shopping district.

Food and drink
Charlotte Corday, 114 rue St-Jean, T02 31 86 33 25, chocolat-corday.fr. Mon 0930-1230, Tue-Sat 0930-1230 and 1400-1900. This treasure house of confectionery and hand-made chocolate indulgences offers a wide selection of local specialities and delightfully inventive treats, to eat now or in smart gift packs.
Stiffler Pâtissier Traiteur, 72 rue St-Jean, T02 31 86 08 94, stifflertraiteur.com. Wed-Sat 0900-1300 and 1430-1930, Sun 0800-1800. Top-quality pastries are the speciality here, and you can sit down and sample them on the premises, which are also a *salon de thé*. In addition, the shop sells ready-prepared meats, salads and savoury dishes to take away.

Markets
There's a produce market somewhere in Caen every day of the week. The city's

biggest market is on Sun morning (0730-1330), when hundreds of stalls fill place Courtonne and neighbouring streets and run 4 rows deep along quai Vendeuvre. This huge gathering of local producers and market traders attracts buyers and browsers from the whole city and outlying areas. Not only is there a huge array of high-quality food, fresh farm produce and farm-made andouilles, cheeses and cider, but also whole sections devoted to hats and clothes, shoes and leather goods, carpets and kitchenware, books and toys and all sorts of arts and crafts.

⚠ What to do

Caen *p24, map p26*
Food and wine
Ferme de Billy, 29 bis rue de l'Eglise, Rots, T02 31 97 32 04, ferme-de-billy.com. Daily 1 Apr-8 Nov, otherwise Mon-Sat. About 7 km from Caen, heading northwest from the city, drop in at this interesting 17th-century mixed farm with 10,000 apple trees. Watch apple juice, ciders, *pommeau* and Calvados being made – and enjoy a free taste. There's also a restaurant, but advance booking is required. Guided tour (1½ hrs) €3.50.

Racing
Hippodrome de Caen, La Prairie, T02 31 27 50 80, hippodrome-caen.com. €3, under 18s free. For lovers of horseracing, Caen's famous 2-km track La Prairie borders the south side of the city centre, beside the north bank of the River Orne. There are about 30 races every year.

Tours
Caen tourist office tours, information and reservation T02 31 27 14 14, tourisme.caen. fr. End Jun-end Aug, Tue-Sat. €6, €4.50 concessions, under 10s free. Caen tourist office runs a range of guided city tours on summer afternoons, including a tour of the Château (starting 1400 and 1630), a walk to the Abbaye aux Dames (1430) and a walk to the Abbaye aux Hommes (1530). Tours last from 1¼ hrs to 1½ hrs, and are in French only. Caen tourist office dramatized tours, information and reservation T02 31 27 14 14, tourisme.caen.fr. Approx 8 Jul-23 Aug. €11-14, concessions €6-10.50, under 10s free. For French speakers, actors bring history to life on walking tours of the Château (Wed, Fri and Sat 1700) or to the Abbaye aux Dames (Thu and Sat 2100). **Petit Train**, leaves from place St-Pierre, opposite the tourist office, T06 16 37 01 45. Jun-Sep, 1000-1800, approx hourly departures. €6, €4 child. Board the 'Little Train' for a gentle trip through the city centre to all the main sights. Commentary is in French and English.

ⓘ Directory

Caen *p24, map p26*
Hospital CHU de Caen, Av de la Côte de Nacre, T02 31 06 31 06, chu-caen.fr. **Pharmacy** One of the most centrally located pharmacies is the **Grande Pharmacie du Progrès**, 2 Blvd des Alliés (corner of place St-Pierre), T02 31 27 90 90, grandepharmacieduprogres.pharminfo.fr. Mon-Sat 0800-2000.

Côte Fleurie

Between the estuaries of the Seine and the Orne, the sandy Calvados coast has been attracting high-class holidaymakers since the 19th century. A century ago the beach resort of Deauville was synonymous with fashionable elegance. Facing it across the River Touques, neighbouring Trouville catered for those respectable people who couldn't quite afford Deauville, and the smaller beachfront communities along the wide sandy seafront made every effort to capture something of the same style. Nowadays, on the Côte Fleurie just as everywhere else, there's a good deal less aristocratic refinement and a more everyday working-town atmosphere. Yet the old glamour has not quite gone, with plenty of well-dressed tourists strolling Deauville's wooden promenade in the short, busy summer season, visiting for a breath of sea air and a flutter at the races.

Strictly speaking, the cliffs east of Trouville belong not to the Côte Fleurie but to the Corniche Normande. At its northern and eastern tip, the picturesque, arty old harbour of Honfleur is one of just two places on this Calvados shore with any great history. The other, on the River Dives at the other end of the Côte, is Dives-sur-Mer. It was from the ancient port of Dives that William the Conqueror set sail to claim the throne of England.

Honfleur → For listings, see pages 39-42.

Pretty-as-a-picture fishing harbour and much-loved haunt of the Impressionists, Honfleur is also a port with a considerable history. From here Samuel Champlain set sail in 1608 with a party of local men to colonize Canada. The centrepiece of the town is its charming Vieux Bassin (Old Harbour), alive with boats tied up against the cobbled quays, busy waterside bars and restaurants, *salons de thé* and art galleries, and all enclosed by tall, narrow buildings dark with slate. At the fortified harbour entrance stands La Lieutenance, the sturdy 16th-century Governor's House. Turn the corner into equally picturesque place Ste-Catherine with the fascinating Eglise Ste-Catherine at its centre. Constructed in Gothic style, but all of timber, not stone – and by shipwrights, not masons – it was built to thank God for the departure of the English at the end of the Hundred Years War. There's some exquisite wood carving inside.

It's a delight to wander the attractive streets of the old town centre, with their cobbles and small half-timbered dwellings. Rue Haute is especially attractive; the imaginative comic artist, writer and composer Erik Satie (1866-1925) was born at No 90, which now houses an entertaining museum about him and his work, known as the **Maisons Satie** ① *entrance is on the other side of the building at 67 bd Charles-V, T02 31 89 11 11, Wed-Mon 1100-1800, 1000-1900 in summer.*

Arriving in Honfleur
Tourist information There is an **Office de Tourisme** ① *Quai Lepaulmier, T02 31 89 23 30, ot-honfleur.fr, Mon-Sat 0930-1230 and 1400-1830 (1700 Jul-Aug, 1800 Oct-Easter), Sun 1000-1230 and 1400-1700 (no midday closing Jul-Aug, Sun mornings only Oct-Easter).*

Musée Eugène Boudin
① *Place Erik Satie, T02 31 89 54 00. 15 Mar-30 Sep Wed-Mon 1000-1200 and 1400-1800, 1 Oct-14 Mar Wed-Mon 1430-1700, Sat-Sun 1000-1200. €5.10 (€5.580 Jul-Sep); €3.40 students, children 10-18, over 60s (€4.30 Jul-Sep); unemployed, professional artists, under 10s free.*
A surprising museum for such a small town, though a fitting one for a place so influential in the development of modern art, the Boudin Museum is renowned for its 19th- and 20th-century collections with a local emphasis. Here are works by Monet, Jongkind, Courbet, Vallotton, Marais, Dufy and a vast number by Boudin himself, who was born in Honfleur and lived here as a child. In addition, the museum displays interesting contemporary Honfleur artists. An ethnographic section is devoted to Normandy's historic regional costumes, furnishings, toys and everyday objects.

Côte de Grace
The modern artists who gathered in Honfleur at the end of the 19th century – among them Pissarro, Cézanne, Corot, Courbet, Sisley, Monet and Boudin – used to climb this slope with their easels to paint, talk and enjoy a simple meal and home-made cider at Mère Toutain's tavern (now the luxury hotel Ferme St-Siméon). From Mont Joli, on the way, views extend over the town and along the Seine. At the top of the Côte de Grace hill a vast panorama opens up, reaching right across the immense estuary. However, things have changed since the 19th century: a large crucifix now dominates the hill, and the view takes in the petrochemical refineries and industry on the far side of the Seine. Close by, the little chapel of Notre-Dame de Grace, originally 11th century, was rebuilt in the 17th century.

Trouville → *For listings, see pages 39-42.*

Although established several years earlier, Trouville eventually lost ground in the 'class' hierarchy to Deauville, its neighbour across the River Touques. That distinction remains to this day, Trouville having a more popular appeal and workaday feel with its busy harbour and fishing quays where *fruits de mer* and the fresh catch are sold. It also has an all-year-round existence, making it perhaps the more agreeable out of season.

Arriving in Trouville
Tourist information Office de Tourisme ① *32 quai Fernand Moureaux, T02 31 14 60 70, trouvillesurmer.org. Sep-Jun daily 1000-1300, 1400-1800 (Sun morning only; closes at 1600 during school holidays); Jul-Aug Mon-Sat 0930-1900, Sun 1000-1700.*

Places in Trouville
The centre of activity, close to the quayside beside the River Touques, extends from the beach to the Pont des Belges, which crosses to Deauville. Grandiose 19th-century seaside villas ranged along the seashore, some designed as mock chateaux, give a flavour of the town's early years. The old wooden boardwalk still lends traditional charm to the wide beach. Near the promenade you'll find the town's casino (see Bars and clubs, page 41) and a very modest aquarium (see below).

More interesting is the Arts and Ethnography Museum, or **Musée de Trouville Villa Montebello** ① *64 rue du Général Leclerc, T02 31 88 16 26, Wed-Mon, €2, concessions €1.50,* housed in one of the old villas. Here is memorabilia of the resort's heyday, as well as an entertaining collection of the colourful post-war French advertising posters of Raymond Savignac (1907-2002). It also hosts numerous temporary art exhibitions. The museum has a separate art gallery on the port quayside, the **Galerie du Musée** ① *32 bd Fernand Moureaux, T02 31 14 92 06, Wed-Mon, free.*

The modest beachside aquarium, **Natur'Aquarium** ① *'Les Planches' Promenade Savignac; Trouville; 102 31 88 46 04; natur-aquarium.fr; Easter-All Saints 1000-1200 and 1400-1830 (Sun afternoon only), All Saints-Easter Fri-Wed 1400-1730 (and 1000-1200 in part of school holidays); €8, €6 child/concessions,* may amuse young children for an hour with its collections of fish, insects and snakes.

Deauville → *For listings, see pages 39-42.*

Arriving in Deauville
Tourist information Office de Tourisme de Deauville ① *112 rue Victor Hugo, T02 31 14 40 00, deauville.org. Mon-Sat 1000-1800, Sun 1000-1300 and 1400-1700, except Jul-Aug and film festival Mon-Sat 0900-1900, Sun 1000-1800.*

The long, wide boardwalk of wooden slats lying on the sand – called Les Planches – gives a lot of old-fashioned charm to Deauville's immense beach. Once frequented by the royal families of Europe, over 100 years later the resort can still claim a certain cachet.

Deauville was laid out as a more refined alternative to Trouville at the suggestion of the Duc de Morny, half-brother of Napoleon III, after he visited the village of Dosville in marshes on the other side of the River Touques, in 1858. His spacious new town was an immediate success. Eugène Boudin's paintings of bourgeois holidaymakers on Trouville and Deauville beaches between 1865-1895 were revolutionary in their day, showing middle-class women at leisure in the open air, the wind catching at their hair and crinolines. They were also among the first ever paintings of families holidaying at a beach resort. It is striking that everyone on the beach, including the children, was fully clothed.

Deauville has few must-see sights, but people-watching is the thing here. There's genuine money on display, especially at the top hotels and the gleaming casino, the racecourse and the yacht marina with its jostling boats. A number of prestigious summer events are held in Deauville – international polo championships, golf tournaments and a horse fair. The Festival du Cinéma Américain (American Film Festival) in early September brings Deauville's summer to a close, but not without excitement as it's not unusual for Hollywood stars to make an appearance.

West of Deauville

The coast road skirts long sandy beaches backed by woods, and passes through the well-kept, sedate resorts of Villers-sur-Mer and Houlgate, where mock-medieval pre-war holiday villas adorn the seafront. Between the two towns, the road heads inland to avoid the steep, dark slopes of the sea-facing Vaches Noires hills, cut into rugged ravines and cliffs noted for their profusion of fossils.

Dives-sur-Mer, the only place along this shore that predates the 19th century, is a historic and picturesque harbour town near the mouth of the River Dives. During the Middle Ages it flourished as a large and important port serving Caen, and there are still some 15th and 16th-century buildings, notably the handsome wooden Halles (covered market). From Dives harbour William the Bastard, Duke of Normandy, set sail with 1000 ships on the voyage that turned him into William the Conqueror, King of England.

Cross the river to enter Cabourg, a smart, purpose-built resort laid out in the middle of the 19th century alongside the wide sandy beach. It follows an interesting plan, with a semi-circle of boulevards radiating from the seafront public gardens, casino and Grand Hotel, which together form the focal point of the town. Although he was quite scathing about the resort, Cabourg is proud of its association with Marcel Proust (the waterfront promenade is named after him), who holidayed here every year from 1907 to 1914.

West of Cabourg, the preserved **Batterie de Merville** ① *place du 9ème Bataillon, Merville-Franceville, T02 31 91 47 53, batterie-merville.com, 0930-1830 (1730 in winter), €6, concessions €3.50*, was one of the formidable gun emplacements and bunkers of Hitler's Atlantic Wall. It controlled the Orne estuary and could fire directly on to Sword Beach. In an operation costing hundreds of lives, it was seized and put out of action by British bombers and paratroops during the night before the D-Day Landings. Part of the bunker, Casemate 1, has been immaculately restored, and is the setting for a noisy, alarmingly realistic re-enactment of the battle several times an hour.

Côte Fleurie listings

For hotel and restaurant price codes and other relevant information, see pages 13-17.

☺ Where to stay

Honfleur *p36*
€€€€-€€€ **La Ferme St-Siméon**, Adolphe-Marais, T02 31 81 78 00, fermesaintsimeon.fr. In its former existence as a modest hostelry run by Mère Toutain, this small hilltop hotel was assured a place in the history of modern art when its regular clientele began to include such artists as Corot, Courbet, Boudin and Monet. Today it is a luxurious country-house-style hotel of tremendous charm and panache, with wood panelling, beams and rich fabrics. It has a pretty garden, dazzling estuary views, traditional comfortable rooms and an excellent restaurant. Facilities include a spa.
€€ **La Ferme de la Grande Cour**, Côte de Grâce, T02 31 89 04 69, fermedelagrande cour.com. This simple, family-run 2-star hotel with wooden beams and rustic decor is well placed near the Notre Dame de Grâce chapel outside Honfleur. Stairs climb to varied, traditional, functional but adequately equipped bedrooms. It has calm and attractive grounds, a restaurant emphasizing fish dishes and the flavours of Normandy, and pleasant outdoor summer dining in the shade of trees.

Chambres d'hôtes
€€€ **La Petite Folie**, -44 rue Haute, T06 74 39 46 46, lapetitefolie-honfleur.com. An unusual chambre d'hôte occupying 2 picturesque old houses in this delightful street, the 'Little Madness' has a sumptuous high-life feel, with quirkily original furnishings, masses of flair and very comfortable, well-equipped rooms. B&B in one house, self-catering in the other.

Trouville *p37*
€€€ **Flaubert**, Gustave Flaubert, T02 31 88 37 23, flaubert.fr. Mid-Feb to mid-Nov. It's possible to stay right on the beachfront at Trouville, in this pleasant and traditional hotel in a 1930s mock-medieval villa, well placed just a few mins' walk from the town centre. Rooms are comfortable and attractive, with pale colours, pictures and antiques. Facilities deserve more than the 2-star rating.

Deauville *p37*
€€€€ **Normandy**, rue Jean Mermoz, T02 31 98 66 22, lucienbarriere.com/en/luxury-hotel/Deauville.html. A superlative example of turn-of-the-century mock-medieval Norman beach-resort architecture, this is a veritable palace of towers and tiles and green-painted timbers, steep roofs and dormer windows. Inside, the Normandy has a smart country-house feel, with every comfort and convenience. Rooms are very richly furnished and decorated. An interior courtyard accommodates the tables of the grand belle epoque restaurant. A covered walkway connects the hotel to the casino.
€€€€ **Royal**, Cornuché, T02 31 98 66 33, lucienbarriere.com/en/luxury-hotel/Deauville.html. Open approx Mar-Oct and 30-31 Dec. This creamy palace with red highlights is the grandest hotel in Deauville, and one of the grandest in France. The bedrooms and suites are opulently furnished and decorated, with luxury wallpapers and carpets, rich drapery and fine furnishings. It has also 2 extremely luxurious restaurants.
€€ **Chantilly**, av de la République, T02 31 88 79 75, hotel-chantilly.com. Deauville on the cheap? No, it's not that cheap, but this comfortable, pleasant little hotel is excellent value. It's close to the racecourse and the main shopping streets.

West of Deauville *p38*
€€€€ Grand Hôtel, Les Jardins du Casino Cabourg, T02 31 91 01 79. The famed seafront **Grand Hôtel de Cabourg**, beside the casino and gardens at the centre of the resort, was once one of the Côte Fleurie's masterpieces of belle epoque style. That glamour has faded into memory, but there are still spacious rooms, sea views and helpful service. Choose the sea-facing side – the other rooms are less pleasing.

❷ Restaurants

Honfleur *p36*
€€ La Ferme St-Siméon, Rue Adolphe-Marais, T02 31 81 78 00, fermesaintsimeon.fr. Lunch and dinner. About 120 years ago artists met at this Côte de Grace inn for plain and simple fare with a glass of cider. Today it's a prestigious Michelin-starred restaurant, with its massive old timbers and brickwork, where traditional local flavours are an important part of the inspiration for refined cooking. Shellfish is the speciality. The *carte des vins* includes some of the grandest wines in France.
€€ Sa Qua Na, 22 place Hamelin, T02 31 89 40 80, alexandre-bourdas.com/saquana. Thu-Sun for lunch and dinner. The name is (broadly) Japanese for 'fish', and that's the speciality of this tranquil, refined establishment. Under chef Alexandre Bourdas, skilful preparations like a piece of sea bream lightly cooked in coconut and lime oil are prepared with delicacy and finesse. The uncluttered ivory and charcoal decor with pale wooden tables enhances the zen-like simplicity. A meal here is a first-rate gastronomic experience. Book well ahead.
€ Bistro des Artistes, 14 place Pierre Berthelot, T02 31 89 95 90. 1200-1400, 1900-2200 (always phone to book). Enjoy simple, cheerful eating at this arty little quayside restaurant just off place Ste-Catherine. On offer is a choice of tasty prepared salads all freshly made when ordered, delicious home-

made bread, fresh oysters or a cooked dish of the day. Decor lives up to the name, with art books to peruse.
€ La Tortue, 30 rue de l'Homme-de-Bois, T02 31 81 24 60, restaurantlatortue.fr. Open daily Apr-Nov. Good-value Normandy eating is served here in one of the town centre's appealing old half-timbered houses. Its different rooms are cosy and attractive with pale wooden floors, painted beams, walls adorned with pictures and white napery on tables that are set close together. There's a choice of wines by the glass to accompany straightforward fish and meat dishes usually well prepared.

Trouville *p37*
Market
At Trouville's daily fish market on the quayside, you can buy ready-to-eat takeaway plates of oysters and other *fruits de mer*, complete with sliced lemon.
€€ Bistrot Les Quatre Chats, 8 rue d'Orléans, T02 31 88 94 94. Mon-Fri 1930-2130 and also Fri-Sun 1200-1330. With its immaculate 1950s decor, this popular and lively brasserie could almost pass for an old cinema, except, of course, for the little tables, snack-bar bench seating, simple traditional French cooking and well-stocked bar.
€€ Les Vapeurs, 160 quai Fernand Moureaux, T02 31 88 15 24, lesvapeurs.fr. Open all day. On the Trouville quayside among several other popular brasseries, Les Vapeurs is a pre-war establishment complete with original fittings. It can be too lively and crowded for comfort, but fresh local fish and shellfish are on the menu, with creamy Normandy sauces, and there's a selection of Normandy cheeses too. Prices are reasonable. During Deauville's film festival, you may see some famous faces.

Cafés
Dupont avec un Thé, 134 bd Fernand Moureaux, T02 31 88 13 82, and 20 place Morny, Deauville, T02 31 88 20 79,

patisseriedupont.com. This most luxurious of *pâtisseries salons de thé* is a feature of the Côte Fleurie, with a branch on both sides of the River Touques. Sit down and enjoy fine chocolate, fruit and almond indulgences or tender *macarons*.

Deauville *p37*
€€ Royal, Bd Cornuché, T02 31 98 66 33, lucienbarriere.com/en/luxury-hotel/ Deauville.html. Mar-Oct, and 30-31 Dec, Mon-Fri dinner, Sat-Sun lunch and dinner. There are 2 opulent, gloriously old-fashioned restaurants in this white palace hotel. The **Etrier** specializes in modern cuisine, while the **Côté Royal**, draped in luxury, offers substantial traditional French set menus.

West of Deauville *p38*
Dupont avec un Thé, 42 rue Gaston Manneville, Dives-sur-Mer, T02 31 91 04 30, and 6 Av Mer, Cabourg, T02 31 24 60 32, patisseriedupont.com. The Côte Fleurie favourite *pâtisserie salon de thé* has tender macarons and delicious treats of chocolate, fruit and almond. There's a branch in both these main towns at the western end of the coast.

🎵 Bars and clubs

Honfleur *p36*
Le Vintage Café, 8 quai des Passagers, T02 31 89 05 28. All day until late, food served Wed-Sun all day till 2400. Convivial, laid-back atmosphere, food, wine and an evening of live jazz is the mix that makes this one of Honfleur's most popular spots for visitors and locals. It's open for snacks and meals during the day too.

Trouville *p37*
Casino Barrière de Trouville, Place du Maréchal Foch, T02 31 87 75 00, lucienbarriere.com. Sun-Thu 1000-0200, Fri 1000-0300, Sat 1000-0400. Over 18s only – ID required. If you'd like a flutter but

don't want to risk losing a bundle among Deauville's high-rollers, try your luck in Trouville instead. Maybe something of a poor relation to Deauville's casino (see below), nevertheless Trouville's grandiose waterfront landmark has many bars and restaurants, more than 200 slot machines and 2 gaming tables.

Deauville *p37*
Casino Barrière de Deauville, 2 rue Edmond-Blanc, T02 31 14 31 14, lucienbarriere.com. Sun-Thu 1000-0200, Fri 1000-0300, Sat 1000-0400. Gaming tables from 1600. Over 18s only – ID required. Deauville has one of the grandest casinos in Europe, a glorious belle epoque palace belonging to the **Lucien Barrière** group (which owns several of the town's classiest addresses). Inside, in sumptuous pre-war gilded settings of chandeliers, marble and rich fabrics, there are slot machines and gaming rooms, 3 restaurants, 3 bars and a nightclub (**Régine's** – see below), a cinema and a show theatre with a wide spectrum of entertainment. The dress code is reasonably smart, with no sportswear allowed.
Le Régine's, Casino Barrière de Deauville, T02 31 14 31 96. Summer daily, out of season Fri-Sat and national holidays only 2300-0500. Dark, art deco designs create the opulent, hedonistic mood of this smart disco and nightclub at Deauville's Casino. Beware: the cheapest drinks on the menu start at €20 a glass (€120 for a bottle).
Les Planches, Domaine du Bois-Lauret, Blonville-sur-Mer, T02 31 87 58 09, lesplanches.com. Daily in summer, out of season Fri-Sat 2300-0500 (sometimes later). Variable entry fees, sometimes free. 7 km along the seafront, this is one of the resort's top spots for a night of upbeat music (mostly house), provided by a resident DJ and often celebrity guest DJs. There is a huge glitzy main space and several other areas including a pool, all right beside the beach.

🛍 Shopping

Honfleur p36
Markets

The town centre around place Ste-Catherine has an excellent street market on Sat mornings, with a tempting array of all the best of Normandy's food and drink.

Trouville p37
Markets

There's a daily indoor fish market at the Poissonnerie, on the waterfront. On Wed and Sun, a busy market runs along the quayside from the Poissonnerie to the Pont des Belges.

⏱ What to do

Trouville p37
Walking tours

Trouville tourist office, 32 quai Fernand Moureaux, T02 31 14 60 70, trouvillesurmer. org. May-Sep. French only. Trouville tourist office puts on varied imaginative guided walking tours of Trouville – for example, a walk on the beach to find local shellfish

Racing

Deauville-Clairefontaine, Route de Clairefontaine, Deauville, T02 31 14 69 00, hippodrome-deauville-clairefontaine.com. Though apparently oriented to holidaymakers and family visits, even encouraging picnickers to its pretty setting, this track is also serious about racing, with steeplechase and other events as well as flat racing every few days throughout the summer.

Deauville-La Touques, 45 Av Hocquart de Turtot, Deauville, T02 31 14 20 00, france-galop.com. Deauville's prestigious main racecourse, almost in the town centre, attracts serious and wealthy racing enthusiasts as well as holiday crowds, especially to its mid-Aug yearling sales. The track holds about 50 races each year, with international meetings in summer and also a Dec season, which is run on a fibre track.

Le Pays d'Auge

Taking up a large part of eastern Calvados (and crossing the border into the Orne *département*), the historic heart of the Pays d'Auge lies between the Touques and Dives rivers. Around its edges are old country towns and marketplaces, notably Pont l'Evêque, St-Pierre-sur-Dives and Orbec. This profoundly rural, gently hilly region of apple orchards, contented cows, stud farms, winding lanes and picture-book villages contains some of Normandy's richest and most satisfying countryside. Here are cottages of heavy timbers, grand old manor houses that local gentry once called home, and traditional little farms and farmyards. Some of France's best known gourmet cheeses come from here, among them Pont l'Evêque, Livarot, Pavé d'Auge and (in the Orne), best known of them all, Camembert. With all those apple orchards, it's no surprise that the Auge is known as well for cider and Calvados. Farm gate signs beckon passersby to sample their home-made products, and for those with time to spare, two marked routes can be followed through the region, the Route du Cidre (cider route) and Route du Fromage (cheese route).

Driving through Le Pays d'Auge

This is a rural ride through one of the loveliest parts of Normandy. The starting point is Pont l'Evêque, one of the little towns that lie around the edges of the Pays d'Auge. It can be reached from Caen (40 km on autoroute A13 or main road D675), or from the Côte Fleurie (8 km from Deauville, 17 km from Honfleur).

Take the smaller rural road (D48) heading upriver on the left bank of the River Touques (in the direction of Lisieux). At the village of **Coquainvilliers**, Calvados Boulard's distillery **Moulin de la Foulonnerie** is open to visitors in summer. Turn right on to D270, left when you reach D45, right again on to D270A at Manerbes. This leads into the heart of the Pays d'Auge. When you reach the former abbey **Abbaye du Val Richer**, transformed into a château in the 19th century, turn right on to D59. Pass another country house, **Château de Roque Baignard**, and follow the D117. Reaching D16, turn left and right towards **Clermont-en-Auge**.

Just 3 km away is **Beuvron-en-Auge**, a picture postcard of a place with its streets of timber-framed cottages. Turn south on D49 (and on to D50), until you reach a left turn for the village of **Cambremer**. Come back and continue (on D101) to **Crèvecœur-en-Auge**, where there is an example of a small well-preserved **medieval château**.

Take D16 to **St-Pierre-sur-Dives** to see its Gothic church and chapter house and covered market place. On a Monday, the town is crowded because of its market. Now turn back towards Lisieux on D511.

One of the attractive features of Pays d'Auge is its old *manoirs* and châteaux of timber, stone and patterned brick. Most of these date from the 16th century. Continue to St-Julien-le-Faucon, where two examples lie just off this road, on the left at **Grandchamp-le-Château**, where the moated château is a fortified house, and on the right at **Coupesarte**, where the manor and its grounds are now a farm. Both are private houses. Continue to Lisieux, the capital of the Pays d'Auge. Avoid the town centre by taking the ring road (D613, D406), following signs back to Pont l'Evêque and the Côte Fleurie, or turn left on D613 if you are going towards Caen.

Pont l'Evêque (13 km inland from Deauville)

Though extensively damaged in 1944, Pont l'Evêque has a bustling, congenial air and an attractive setting at the meeting of rivers. It gives its name to one of the most famous of Normandy's strong, creamy cheeses, made and sold here for 900 years, and is known too for its Calvados. There is a tourist **information office** ① *16 bis rue St Michel, T02 31 64 12 77, blangy-pontleveque.com.*

Despite the damage of 1944, the old town has a few handsome half-timbered houses as a reminder of its pre-war appearance, for example along the rue St-Michel (the main street) and its continuation rue de Vaucelles. A side turn leads to the fine Flamboyant Gothic Eglise St-Michel. Along here too you'll find the grand brick and stone 18th-century Hôtel de Brilly, now housing the town hall and tourist office. At their distillery in town, Calvados-makers Père Magloire run the charming Museum of Calvados and Old Crafts, or **Musée du Calvados et des Métiers Anciens** ① *route de Trouville, T02 31 64 30 31, calvados-pere-magloire.com, €3.*

Le Pays d'Auge listings

For hotel and restaurant price codes and other relevant information, see pages 13 17.

🛏 Where to stay

Pont l'Evêque *p44*
€€€-€€ Le Lion d'Or, place du Calvaire, T02 31 65 01 55, leliondorhotel.com.
Right in the centre of the little town, this attractive well-run family-owned small hotel has character and charm and offers comfortable, well-equipped rooms of a good size and decorated with simple, elegant taste. The 'duplex' rooms are like home-from-home apartments. There's free Wi-Fi, breakfast is good value, and the hotel also has its own little spa area with a variety of relaxation treatments.

🛍 Shopping

Pont l'Evêque *p44*
Market
Mon morning.

⚑ What to do

Le Pays d'Auge *p43*
Distillery visits
To see Calvados, cider and pommeau being made, and enjoy a taste of it too, these traditional Pays d'Auge distilleries in Calvados are open to visitors:
Calvados Père Magloire, de Trouville, Pont l'Evêque, T02 31 64 30 31, calvados-pere-magloire.com.
Apr-Oct. 45-min guided tour, €3.
Christian Drouin, Cœur de Lion, Coudray-Rabut (2 km from Pont l'Evêque), T02 31 64 30 05, coeur-de-lion.com. Mon-Sat 0900-1200, 1400-1800. Free (including tasting).

Bayeux

One of Normandy's most pleasing country towns, and with more historical significance than most, Bayeux is a place to stroll, explore and linger. It has good restaurants, especially on and around the main street rue St-Martin and its continuation rue St-Jean. Its cobbled shopping streets and riverside walks, the wealth of centuries-old half-timbered houses, and the picturesque area around the Norman Gothic cathedral all come as a surprise so close to the Landing Beaches – for which it makes an ideal base. During the Second World War the Germans deployed most of their troops defending Caen and were unable to put up strong resistance at Bayeux and as a result, it was the first French town to be liberated, and largely kept its pre-war appearance. On the ring road, the Battle of Normandy Memorial Museum records the events of the invasion and the neighbouring Bayeux War Cemetery is the largest Second World War British Commonwealth war grave in France. Most of the dead fell during the landings on Gold Beach.

The name of Bayeux is, of course, synonymous with its greatest possession – the fascinating 900-year-old Bayeux Tapestry, beautifully displayed in the town centre. This single strip of cloth superbly illustrates the long and close association between Normandy and England.

Arriving in Bayeux

Tourist information
Pole Touristique du Bessin ① *Pont St-Jean, T02 31 51 28 28, bayeux-bessin-tourisme.com, Jul-Aug Mon-Sat 0900-1900, Sun 0900-1300 and 1400-1800. Otherwise Mon-Sat 0930-1230 and 1400-1800, Sun 1000-1300, 1400-1800 (Nov-Mar closes at 1730).*

Places in Bayeux → *For listings, see page 48.*

Musée de la Tapisserie de Bayeux (Bayeux Tapestry Museum)
① *Centre Guillaume le Conquérant, rue de Nesmond, T02 31 51 25 50, tapisserie-bayeux. fr.Ticket desk open 15 Mar-15 Nov 0900-1745 (May-Aug until 1815), 16 Nov-14 Mar (except Jan) 0930-1145 and 1430-1715, closed Jan, museum closes 45 mins after ticket desk closes. €9, €4 concessions and children, under 10s free.*
As an artwork no less than as a historical document, the Bayeux Tapestry is a phenomenal and unique object, a 900-year-old seamless embroidery telling the tale of one of the most important events in European history. Its full length (70 m) is displayed so that you can study each of its 72 scenes in turn, as they show with Latin captions how William's inheritance of the throne of England was disputed, his setting out to claim it, the battle at Hastings in which Harold was killed, and William's eventual conquest. It is uncertain, but probable, that the tapestry (technically an embroidery) was commissioned by the 11th-century Bishop Odon of Bayeux and made for him in England. However, it seems it remained in storage until 1476, when it at last decorated the nave of Bayeux Cathedral.

Musée Mémorial de la Bataille de Normandie (Memorial Museum of the Battle of Normandy)
① *Bd Fabian Ware, T02 31 51 46 90. Oct-Apr 1000-1230 and 1400-1800, May-Sep 0930-1830, last admission 1 hr before closing. €7; concessions €4.50, children €3.80, veterans free.*
With masses of authentic equipment, artefacts, plans, photographs and documentation of the period, with tableaux and models, and a 25-minute film using archive footage, the museum tells the story of the dramatic Battle of Normandy, which started with the D-Day Landings and ended in victory for the Allies on 29 August 1944.

Bayeux War Cemetery
① *Bd Fabian Ware. It is difficult to park outside the cemetery, but nearby chemin des Marettes generally has space.*
This is the largest British Commonwealth wartime cemetery in France, with the graves of 4144 British dead and more than 500 others, mainly German. Across the road, the Bayeux Memorial bears the names of over 1800 other British Commonwealth troops missing in action whose bodies were not recovered. Most of the dead were killed as they arrived on Gold Beach or in the first days of the liberation.

Bayeux listings

For hotel and restaurant price codes and other relevant information, see pages 13-17.

☺ Where to stay

Bayeux *p46*

€€€ Churchill, 16 rue St-Jean, T02 31 21 31 80, hotel-churchill.fr. Centrally located in an attractive stone building on a cobbled shopping street near place de Québec, this well-run 3-star is a good base for visiting the town or exploring further afield. Rooms are moderately sized, but well equipped and attractively decorated and furnished. Those at the back are quieter. Staff are helpful.

€€€ Lion d'Or, rue St-Jean, T02 31 92 06 90, liondor-bayeux.fr. This handsome old former coaching inn is a calm, reasonably priced, family-run 3-star **Relais du Silence** with a plush, luxurious feel. Arranged around a courtyard, the bedrooms are mainly on the small side, traditional and comfortable, and pleasantly decorated in classic taste. Choose a suite for more space. The hotel has an excellent restaurant.

€€ Argouges, rue St-Patrice, T02 31 92 88 86, hotel-dargouges.com. In a pair of rather grand 17th-century buildings set back from the street, some bedrooms and public areas at this inexpensive 2-star hotel have period features and a château-like feel. The setting is surprisingly peaceful for such a convenient location in the city centre. Breakfast might be considered overpriced.

€ Auberge de Jeunesse, 39 rue Général de Dais, T02 31 92 55 72, www.bayeux-familyhome.com. With a range of basic hotel rooms as well as shared rooms in a 17th-century town centre house, and cheaper dormitory accommodation in a separate building on the edge of town if you prefer, this popular youth hostel has plenty of charm with its paved courtyard, clean and unpretentious amenities, free breakfast and low-cost dinner.

🍴 Restaurants

Bayeux *p46*

€€ Le Pommier, 30-40 rue des Cuisiniers, T02 31 21 52 10, restaurantlepommier.com. Daily 1200-1400 and 1900-2100 (Nov-Mar closed Sun). As if the name didn't say it all, the apple-themed decor and colours make sure there's no mistaking the speciality of this stylish restaurant near the cathedral. Normandy's traditional dishes are imaginatively prepared and attractively served in an atmospheric setting of beams and bare stone. Tables are a little close together. There's also a vegetarian menu, if preferred.

€€ Lion d'Or, 71 rue St-Jean, T02 31 92 06 90, liondor-bayeux.fr. Lunch and dinner. Traditional and plush decor in this old inn provide the civilized setting for well-prepared classic French cuisine. Work through the menu régional, with Normandy specialities in every course.

€ Cafélnn, 67 rue St-Martin, T02 31 21 11 37, cafeinn-bayeux.com. Mon-Sat 0900-1900. This little *épicerie*, coffee shop and *salon de thé* is just the place to relax with a coffee and pastry, and also makes a good choice for inexpensive snacks, salads and omelettes at very modest prices.

Les Plages du Débarquement (Landing Beaches)

The Allied invasion of Nazi Europe started early one summer morning with the surprise appearance from the sea of 160,000 soldiers along on the wide sandy beaches of western Calvados and the eastern Cotentin. It was one of the most thrilling, astounding and shocking events in the history of warfare. Codenamed Operation Neptune, the landings took place over a 80-km stretch of coast, divided into five separate areas of attack, codenamed (west to east) Utah, Omaha, Gold, Juno and Sword. The Americans took on Utah and Omaha, British forces landed on Gold and Sword beaches and Canadian troops went ashore at Juno. As they surged from their vessels into the water and waded towards the gunfire, large numbers of the young conscripts were mown down in their first steps. It remains difficult to grasp the magnitude of what the men endured, the greatness of what they achieved, and the vastness of the profligate destruction which ensued, of whole towns and villages, cathedrals and cottages, livelihoods and lives, that were lost before the final victory. Today the Landing Beaches are simply wide airy sands fringed in places with the promenades of little holiday resorts and fishing ports, yet all along this shore numerous memorials honour those who died here, and those who lived, on 6 June 1944.

Visiting Les Plages du Débarquement (Landing Beaches)

Getting there
The two best bases for a tour of the Landing Beaches are Caen and Bayeux. Both are easily accessible by train from Paris (Caen about 90 minutes, Bayeux two hours). If you are including Utah Beach on your trip, choose Bayeux.

Getting around
Although there are some local bus services in the Landing Beaches area, they are impractical for touring. It's best to join an organized minibus tour, for example with Le Mémorial in Caen (memorial-caen.fr), or pre-book a rental car to be collected on your arrival.

Tourist information
Arromanches-les-Bains ① *2 rue Maréchal Joffre, T02 31 22 36 45, arromanches.com.* **Carentan** (Manche département) ① *boulevard de Verdun, T02 33 71 23 50, ot-carentan.fr.* **Courseulles-sur-Mer** ① *5 rue du 11 Novembre, T02 31 37 46 80, courseulles-sur-mer.com.* **Grandcamp-Maisy** ① *118 rue Aristide Briand, T02 31 22 62 44, isigny-grandcamp-intercom.com.* **Isigny-sur-Mer** ① *16 rue Emile Demagny, T02 31 21 46 00, isigny-grandcamp-intercom.com.* **Lion-sur-Mer** ① *place du 18 Juin 1940, T02 31 96 87 95, mairie-lion-sur-mer.fr.* **Luc-sur-Mer** ① *rue du Docteur Charcot, T02 31 97 32 71, luc-sur-mer.fr.* **Ouistreham-Riva-Bella** ① *Jardins*

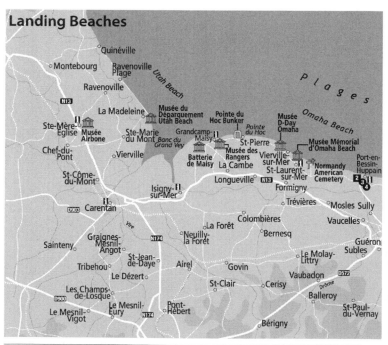

Landing Beaches

du Casino, T02 31 97 18 63, ouistreham.fr/office. **Port-en-Bessin-Huppain** ① *quai Baron Gérard, T02 31 22 45 80, bessin-normandie.com*. **St-Aubin-sur-Mer** ① *Digue Favreau, T02 31 97 30 41, tourisme-saintaubinsurmer.fr*. **St-Laurent-sur-Mer** (Omaha Beach)① *Seafront, rue Désiré Lemière, T07 87 79 74 21, oti-omaha.fr*. **Ste-Mère-Eglise** (Manche département) ① *6 rue Eisenhower, T02 33 21 00 33, sainte-mere-eglise.info*.

A multimedia GPS video-guide for Ste-Mère-Eglise and Utah Beach is available from Ste-Mère-Église tourist office, see above. Grandly called Musée à Ciel Ouverte (Open Skies Museum), it allows you to find, visit and explore 12 sites connected to the local D-Day landings. The guide costs €8 per day, but there is a €250 deposit.

Sword Beach and Pegasus Bridge → For listings, see pages 58-59.

Sword Beach

About 8 km long and centred on the small resort of Lion-sur-Mer, Sword stretched from the Riva Bella beach near Ouistreham harbour on the Orne estuary almost to St-Aubin-sur-Mer. Today, nearly its whole length is a ribbon development of holiday towns, protected by a sea wall and fronting on to wide flat sands under big skies. A few remnants of German beach defences are still in place.

The plan for the British troops who came ashore here on D-Day was to travel inland and meet up with the men of the airborne division who had already successfully taken control

D-Day

The phrase 'D-Day' (Jour-J in French) does not refer specifically to the Normandy Landings. It is military parlance for the day on which a major operation is planned to start. The phrase 'H-Hour' is used for the exact time. The intended start date for Operation Neptune was 5 June, not the 6th, but it was held up by the weather. So the landings took place on 'D-Day plus one'.

of the bridges over the Caen canal (Pegasus Bridge) and Orne river, and proceed from there to Caen. Resistance on the beach was lighter than anticipated, and the men made their way cautiously towards the bridges.

The village of Colleville-Montgomery, just inland, was the site of a German underground bunker, signal centre and gun emplacement (restored, and can be visited). Soldiers of the Suffolk Regiment went into action and proceeded to capture it. Later, the village adopted the name of the commander of the British forces to show gratitude.

Further inland though, the British troops were stopped in their tracks by Panzer tank divisions who put up a powerful defence and prevented the British advance to Caen.

Pegasus Bridge

On the busy main road (D515) from the city of Caen to its seaport at Ouistreham, a turning (D514) crosses on to the bridge over the Caen canal. This small bridge saw the first action of the Normandy Invasion, preparing the way for D-Day the following morning, and became known as Pegasus Bridge in honour of the British troops of the Oxfordshire and Buckinghamshire Light Infantry (Ox and Bucks) Airborne; their insignia is the mythical winged horse Pegasus. Under the command of Major John Howard, some hours before dawn on 6 June 1944 they landed in three gliders almost beside the bridge. Their mission was to capture the bridge intact, while another group took the nearby River Orne crossing. This was successfully achieved in just 10 minutes, though with loss of life. The men then used the premises of the Café Gondrée, next to the bridge, to tend to their wounds. The bridge itself was replaced in 1994. The original Pegasus Bridge can now be seen outside the museum of the **Mémorial Pegasus** ① *av du Major Howard, Ranville, T02 31 78 19 44, normandie1944.fr, Feb-Nov, approx 0930-1830, €6.50, €4.50 child and concessions*, just across the canal.

Musée du Mur de l'Atlantique (Atlantic Wall Museum)

① *Av 6 Juin, Ouistreham, T02 31 97 28 69, musee-grand-bunker.com. Apr-Sep 0900-1900, Oct-Mar (except Jan, closed) 1000-1800. €7, €5 6-12 years, under 6s free.*
With impressive authentic and original interiors, and a sweeping view of Sword Beach, this museum occupies the immaculately restored 17-m-tall concrete German HQ which commanded the River Orne defences.

Atlantikwall

The massive German gun emplacements and batteries along the Normandy coast were part of the Atlantikwall. The Germans realized early in their occupation of Europe that the Channel coast was vulnerable to a sea-borne attack and in 1942 Hitler ordered that a continuous line of fire be put in place, reinforced by impenetrable defences, along the continent's entire western coastline. The one weakness in this colossal fortification was that defences were especially focused around ports, as it was thought to be impossible to launch a full-scale attack on Nazi Europe without a harbour to unload men and equipment.

Juno Beach → For listings, see pages 58-59

Canadians had already suffered demoralizing losses on the Normandy coast in the ill-fated Dieppe Raid of 1942. For Operation Neptune, under British command, they were given the 6 km from St-Aubin-sur-Mer to Courseulles-sur-Mer. In the event, despite a difficult approach among offshore rocks and mines, they quickly overcame the German defenders and progressed inland. By 16 June 1944 the area was safe enough for King George V and Prime Minister Winston Churchill to make a brief visit, when they inspected Graye-sur-Mer, adjoining Courseulles. Today, the area is popular for sailing, surfing, horse riding and the sport of *char à voile* – sail-powered go-karting on the flat sands. At low tide, seafood enthusiasts can gather their own shrimps and crabs.

Centre Juno Beach

ⓘ *Voie des Français Libres, Courseulles-sur-Mer, T02 31 37 32 17, junobeach.org. Apr-Sep 0930-1900, Mar and Oct 1000-1800, Feb, Nov and Dec 1000-1700. €7, €5.50 child and concessions, free for veterans and their widows.*

Located on the extreme western end of Juno Beach, this is the only specifically Canadian museum and memorial on the Landing Beaches. It pays tribute to the French and English Canadians who took part in D-Day, including those who had behind-the-scenes roles. It also explores Canada's Anglo-French (and First Nation) culture and history.

Gold Beach → For listings, see pages 58-59.

The centre of attention for most British visitors now, Gold was an 8-km length of coast from near Courseulles-sur-Mer to the rockier shore just west of Arromanches-les-Bains, a resort village on a lightly curved section of beach close to a small rocky headland. Still visible in the water and lying on the beach at Arromanches and Le Hamel about 1 km east are the remnants of the Mulberry Harbour – a fully functioning port assembled on the spot by the Allied forces with ready-made sections towed from England. It was in use just three days after D-Day. After securing the shore and constructing the harbour, the Allies were able to bring ships here from England loaded with soldiers, weapons, equipment and supplies. A beachside D-Day Museum in the heart of busy little Arromanches, right beside these great slabs, explores the story of the Landings and the role and construction of the Mulberry. The Mulberry Harbour at Arromanches was not the only one, however. Two of the ready-made ports, constructed of hollow concrete breakwaters, were towed in sections across the Channel from 6-7 June and were ready for use by 9 June. 'Mulberry A' was assembled at Omaha Beach and served its purpose for just 10 days until broken up by a violent storm on 19 June. 'Mulberry B' at nearby Arromanches survived the storm and became known as Port Winston. During a 10-month period it was used to bring over two million soldiers and half a million armoured vehicles to Normandy, together with all their supplies.

The best overview of the layout of the huge harbour is from the specially constructed viewpoint on the hill rising behind the little town. Signposted 'Belvédère', it is close to the Arromanches 360 cinema.

The coastline remains little developed to this day, and gives a sense of what the British troops themselves saw on the morning of 6 June 1944. Here they were set down with the order to take control of Arromanches, and disable the German gun battery at nearby Longues-sur-Mer. Tanks and armoured vehicles were driven directly on to the beach. An unlikely spot for an invasion, the Arromanches coast was not especially well protected. Although offshore defences had caused damage, on land the German divisions tasked with defending it were not crack troops, while some turned out to be forced labour from Russia and Poland, who had no wish to help their masters. A unit trained to respond to an invasion were unprepared and were in Bayeux. On the coast at Le Hamel, the Germans were not in bunkers but in fortified beach houses that were destroyed by naval bombardment before the troops came ashore.

By the end of that day 25,000 British soldiers had landed on this beach, and the troops had reached several kilometres inland where they met with the Canadians coming in from Juno Beach. In the other direction, they had taken the gun battery at Longues and reached the road above Port-en-Bessin in an effort to aid the Americans battling on a blood-soaked Omaha Beach.

Arromanches 360
① *Chemin du Calvaire, Arromanches les Bains, T02 31 06 06 44, arromanches360.com. Opening and closing times slightly varied every few weeks. Generally open approx 1000-1800 (may be closed Mon part of Nov, part of Feb and part of Oct) €4.90, €4.40 concessions (veterans free), under 10s free. You also have to pay €2 to park in the car park.*
On a hill behind the town, this unusual cinema-in-the-round shows a film called *The Price of Freedom*. Splicing vivid contemporary D-Day footage with modern film of the locations it powerfully brings home the events of D-Day and a sense of its purpose and accomplishment.

Musée du Débarquement (D-Day Museum)
① *Place du 6 juin, T02 31 22 34 31, musee-arromanches.fr. Approx opening times liable to variation Feb and Nov-Dec 1000-1230 and 1330-1700, Mar and Oct 0930-1230 and 1330-1730, Apr 0900-1230, 1230-1800, May-Aug 0900-1900, Sep 0900-1800 (except Sun, opens at 1000), apart from Easter weekend 0900-1900. €7.50, €5.50 child and concessions.*
Dominating the little main street beside the beach, and with real armaments and weaponry standing outside, the museum is right in front of pieces of the Mulberry harbour lying on the sand. Inside, photos, film footage and authentic mementos are displayed, and an extensive scale model shows the scene on D-Day. Audio-visual presentations (in English and other languages) give an insight into the strategy behind D-Day and the engineering feat involved in creating the artificial harbour.

Longues-sur-Mer German Battery

① *Signposted from Longues-sur-Mer. Free.*

A key element in the German defences of the Calvados coast was this massive gun emplacement behind the coast just west of Arromanches, complete with an observation post set into the cliffs. Its four powerful 150-mm guns were able to hit targets not only at sea but also on both Gold Beach and Omaha Beach. In the run-up to D-Day, a British warship engaged it in a determined exchange of fire. Although damaged, it was still in action on the morning of D-Day, but was taken later in the day. The guns are still in place and parts of the bunker are well preserved.

Port-en-Bessin

In between Gold and Omaha beaches, Port-en-Bessin rewards a visit. More correctly called Port-en-Bessin-Huppain (it's administratively joined to neighbouring Huppain), it is known locally simply as Port. A semicircle of granite jetties shelters this charming little fortified fishing village between the cliffs, where there's a daily auction of fresh fish. The village has some good places to eat or to stay. On D-Day, the Americans on Omaha and British on Gold were supposed to meet up at Port-en-Bessin. They managed it on 8 June – two days after the landings.

Omaha Beach → *For listings, see pages 58-59.*

The focus of the American attack was the coast between Vierville-sur-Mer to a point east of Colleville-sur-Mer. Today, at low tide locals stroll the shore calmly gathering shellfish. The rustic Bessin countryside inland is a dense patchwork of small fields and mature hedges. All is utterly peaceful. Yet as soon as you see the layout of Omaha Beach, the problems become clear: the wide, flat beach is hemmed in by a sea wall and cliffs. To leave it requires a steep climb.

The whole of the 20-km stretch of Calvados coast between Port-en-Bessin and the mouth of the River Vire was robustly defended by the Germans, with concrete gun emplacements and smaller gun bunkers. Many can still be seen, dug into the ridge of rocky cliffs rising up and overlooking the seashore. Despite the pounding they received and the passage of time since, some of these concrete structures seem little damaged. From these vantage points the Germans trained their guns on to the wet sand as the American soldiers emerged from their landing craft.

Omaha Beach was bound to be a tough fight and the Americans offered to take it on. But it was even tougher than expected. Delayed after a rough crossing in which most of their armoured vehicles had been lost, they were subjected to a ceaseless torrent of gunfire as they struggled to wade ashore. Many were killed on the spot. Those who reached the cliffs had to climb them with rope ladders. Any who survived the climb found themselves surrounded by landmines. They continued towards the German gun bunkers, which eventually were overrun and silenced. By the evening of the day, the Americans had landed 34,000 men and suffered 2400 casualties, but they had taken control of the awesome German gun emplacement at Pointe-du-Hoc, and at Vierville they held the coast road (D514) to Grandcamp-Maisy in one direction and Port-en-Bessin in the other. For a realistic dramatization of the landings at Omaha Beach, see the opening sequences of Steven Spielberg's film *Saving Private Ryan*.

The area remains deeply marked by the immense American self-sacrifice. Its most affecting sight is the tranquil and neatly kept **Cimetière et Mémorial Américains de**

Normandie (American Military Cemetery and Memorial) ① *signposted 1 km off D514 between St Laurent-sur-Mer and Colleville-sur-Mer, T02 31 51 62 00, abmc.gov/cemeteries/ cemeteries/no.php, daily 0900-1800 (1700 from 16 Sep to 14 Apr) except 25 Dec and 1 Jan,* set back from the beach at the centre of the battlefield. On land given by France to the United States, it holds 9387 graves. In pristine white rows stand the thousands of white crosses, and some Stars of David, laid out before a dignified semi-circular memorial wall on which are inscribed the 1557 names of the missing.

Normandy American Cemetery Visitor Center
① *American Military Cemetery and Memorial, near St Laurent-sur-Mer, T02 31 51 62 00. Same times as cemetery, see above. Free.*
Within the grounds of the cemetery, in a wooded area close to the memorial wall and garden, the centre is one of the most powerful of the D-Day museums. It provides a gripping and vivid view of Operation Overlord, the events of D-Day and what led up to them, and the experience of those who took part, with authentic personal stories, photos and film.

Musée Mémorial d'Omaha Beach (Omaha Beach Memorial Museum)
① *Les Moulins, av de la Libération, St Laurent-sur-Mer, T02 31 21 97 44, musee-memorial-omaha.com. 15 Feb-15 Mar 1000-1230 and 1430-1800, 16 Mar-15 May and 16 Sep-15 Nov 0930-1830, 16 May-30 Jun and 1 Sep-15 Sep 0930-1900, Jul-Aug 0930-1930. €6, €4.70 child 16-18 and up to 25 in full-time education, €3.50 child 7-15, under 7s free.*
Set back 100 m from the beach, the museum displays large collections of authentic D-Day weapons and vehicles, uniforms, personal possessions, maps, photos and more.

Musée D-Day Omaha (Omaha D-Day Museum)
① *Route de Grandcamp-Maisy, Vierville-sur-Mer, T02 31 21 71 80, dday-omaha.org. Open Apr-Oct generally about 1000-1800, except Jun-Aug 0930-1830. €5.70, €3 child and concessions, under 7s free.*
This fascinating small collection of original military material, housed in and around a wartime beachside hangar, includes landing craft and a steel observation dome. Close by, on the same theme, are remnants of the ill-fated Omaha Beach Mulberry Harbour.

Grandcamp-Maisy
This quiet little fishing port and yacht harbour about 10 km along the coast from Omaha Beach was a focal point for German defences around the Banc du Grand Vey bay, a huge area of sandflats between the Calvados coast and the Cotentin peninsula covered at every tide. Two large bunkers complete with underground offices and stores and powerful gun batteries were dug into the coastal cliffs nearby. They could fire on to both Omaha and Utah beaches. One of them, east of Grandcamp-Maisy on the lofty Pointe du Hoc headland (about an hour's walk from the road), was taken by the elite US Rangers force after a ferocious fight on D-Day. On 9 June the Rangers captured the huge underground complex southwest of Grandcamp-Maisy at the **Batterie de Maisy** ① *route des Perruques, T06 78 04 56 25, maisybattery.com, phone to verify times and fee, approx Mar-Sep 1000-1800, Oct-Apr 1000-1600, €5,* which was left abandoned after the war. It was rediscovered and uncovered almost intact by a British enthusiast, Gary Sterne, as he researched the area almost 60 years later. In the village, the **Musée des Rangers** (Rangers Museum) ① *quai Crampon, Grandcamp-Maisy, T02 31 92 33 51, 15 Feb-30 Apr Tue-Sun 1300-1800; May-Oct*

Tue-Sun 1000-1300, 1430-1830 (closed Tue morning). €4.40, €3.30 child and concessions (veterans free), tells the story of the US Rangers and their hair-raisingly difficult and dangerous assaults on the German bunkers.

Utah Beach → *For listings, see pages 58-59.*

Unlike the other Landing Beaches, Utah Beach is not in Calvados but across the Banc du Grand Vey on the Cotentin Peninsula. By sea, it is 20 km from Omaha Beach.

D-Day really began not at dawn, but at 0230 on 6 June, and the invasion came not by sea but from the air. That's the moment when thousands of men of US 101st Airborne descended on the village of Ste-Mère-Eglise, to prepare the way for troops who would be reaching Utah Beach later in the morning. At Ste-Mère-Eglise (see page 50), the events of that night are brought to life at the Musée Airborne. One of the American parachutists was caught on the church tower in the village centre. He is commemorated to this day by a dummy and parachute still hanging there. The Allies needed to move through the Cotentin to capture the port of Cherbourg as soon as possible, and that was the mission of the American soldiers put ashore on Utah Beach. Unlike the tragedy of Omaha Beach, here things went relatively well for the invaders.

Today, the long straight Utah Beach, edged by a low sea wall, is wide, sandy, sparsely inhabited, and remains almost completely undeveloped. Cotentin locals drive here to enjoy the open spaces, for seashore horse riding and sand-karting. Some German defences are still in place. At the southern end of the beach stands a memorial and monument to those who took part in the Landings. You'll notice the KM00 milestone, too, marking the start of the Voie de Liberté (Liberty Trail), which continues 1446 km all the way from here to Bastogne, in Belgium.

Musée du Débarquement Utah Beach (Utah Beach Landing Museum)
ⓘ *La Madeleine, Ste-Marie-du-Mont, T02 33 71 53 35, utah-beach.com. Apr, May, Oct 1000-1800, Jun-Sep 0930-1900, Feb, Mar, Nov 1000-1730. Last entry 1 hr before closing. €7.50, €5.50 concessions, €3 child.*
Located right next to the sand at one end of Utah Beach, beside the Navy memorial, this museum uses authentic artefacts, archives and personal memorabilia to recall the Utah Beach landings. In front of the museum stands an original US landing craft. That alone brings home something of what the troops endured.

Les Plages du Débarquement (Landing Beaches) listings

For hotel and restaurant price codes and other relevant information, see pages 13-17.

🛏 Where to stay

Luc-sur-Mer *p51, map p50*
Campsites
€ Camping Municipal 'La Capricieuse', l'Ecuyer, T02 31 97 34 43, campinglacapricieuse.com. This 4-star campsite in the thriving little resort of Luc-sur-Mer, close to the sands of Sword and Juno beaches, has chalets and mobile homes as well as camping sites. There are adequate facilities, as well as entertainment in season.

Arromanches-les-Bains *p53, map p50*
€€ La Marine, quai du Canada, T02 31 22 34 19, hotel-de-la-marine.fr. There's bright, fresh decor and plenty of blue and white contrasts at this very well-placed traditional waterside hotel at the heart of the tiny resort. It's just a few paces from the D-Day Landings Museum.

Port-en-Bessin *p55, map p50*
€€€€ La Chenevière, on D6, T02 31 51 25 25, lacheneviere.com. Mar-Oct. This sumptuous mansion in a setting of lawns and gardens started as an 18th-century manor house, became grander in the 19th century, and was beautifully restored in the 1980s. Today it has elegant, richly furnished rooms combining antique furnishings with contemporary, and with all modern comforts. There is also a good restaurant.

🍴 Restaurants

Pegasus Bridge *p52, map p50*
€ Pegasus Bridge Café Gondrée, 12 av Commdt Kieffer, Bénouville, T02 31 44 62 25. When the British paratroops landed, they discovered a simple café-bar right beside the

Caen canal bridge (on the Allied side on the canal). The café, flag-draped, is still run by the same family. Ordinary bar fare of drinks, snacks and light meals is served. Inside, it is a veritable museum dedicated to the wartime events. The original Pegasus Bridge can be seen in the nearby Mémorial Pegasus.

Arromanches-les-Bains *p53, map p50*
€€ La Marine, 1 quai du Canada, T02 31 22 34 19, hotel-de-la-marine.fr. A great place to enjoy fresh fish and seafood platters at bay windows or open-air tables right beside the seashore at Gold Beach, within a few mins' walk of the D-Day Museum.
€€ Le Bistro d'Arromanches, 23 rue du Maréchal Joffre, T02 31 22 31 32, le-bistro. fr. Wed-Sun. There's simple, relaxed and cosy decor and good hearty eating of *fruits de mer* and fish dishes, and a good selection of salads, and pizzas, all at reasonable prices, as well as a choice of beers.
€€ Le Bistrot d'à Côte, 12 rue Michel Lefournier, Port-en-Bessin-Huppain, T02 31 51 79 12. There's a seaside feeling at this bright and cheerful bistro near the beach, serving generous, well-prepared traditional fresh fish and seafood dishes with plenty of local flavours.
€€ Le Vauban, 6 rue Nord, Port-en-Bessin-Huppain, T02 31 21 74 83, restaurant-levauban.com. Thu-Mon 1200-1345 and 1900-2045, Tue-Wed 1200-1345. This simple local restaurant, decorated in pale colours with traditional table settings, offers good *fruits de mer*, fresh fish dishes and cuisine based on what's best in the market.

🍸 Bars and clubs

Luc-sur-Mer *p51, map p50*
Casino de Luc-sur-Mer, 20 rue Guynemer, Luc-sur-Mer, T02 31 97 32 19, luc.groupe tranchant.com. Daily 1000-0300, except gaming tables Wed-Sun 2100-0300. It's a

surprise to find cabaret and dancing on the Landing Beaches. Unwind with dinner and a show at the bars, theatre and gaming tables of the seafront casino in this busy little resort.

⚫ What to do

Les Plages du Débarquement (Landing Beaches) *p49, map p50*
Tours
D-Day Tours, 6 rue St-Jean, Bayeux, T02 31 51 70 52, normandywebguide.com. Half-day prices from about €45 per person,

reductions for students. One of several companies offering a choice of full-day and half-day guided tours by minibus to the different beaches. Private guided tours are available. Start in either Caen or Bayeux.

Mémorial de Caen Battlefield Tours, Le Mémorial de Caen, esplanade Général Eisenhower, Caen, T02 31 06 06 45, memorial-caen.fr/fr/circuit_tour. Day trip €111. The Mémorial runs its own 5-hr minibus tour, which includes a visit to the Mémorial de Caen followed by a tour of the Landing Beaches. Tours start out from an assembly point at Caen railway station.

Contents

Cotentin & Mont-St-Michel

Cherbourg-Octeville

In the peaceful post-war years, Cherbourg-Octeville became a major cross-channel ferry port, and today is visited by more yachts than any other harbour in Europe. There is a bustling, enjoyable atmosphere in the old town centre as well as an attractive waterfront plaza, some pedestrianized streets lined with attractive old stone buildings, pleasant cafés and good shops. The marina and town centre lie on the west bank of the harbour, while the ferries and commercial shipping are kept on the east bank. You can still see, though, that Cherbourg-Octeville, with its mighty harbour defences, has a military heritage. Indeed, it's still one of France's largest naval ports. Cherbourg-Octeville originally sprang from an idea in the mind of the 17th-century military architect Marquis de Vauban. His vision was of a fortified trading and naval port at the very tip of the Cotentin, greatly enlarged by man-made harbours, which could be made suitable for large ocean-going vessels. The idea was far ahead of its time. A breakwater strong enough to make this possible could not be built for 150 years, the naval port finally opening in 1858, long after Vauban's death. The town's heyday came in the 1930s, when the largest and most luxurious ocean cruise ships, as well as a huge tonnage of industrial shipping, were docking at Cherbourg. During the Normandy Invasion in 1944, Cherbourg was the centre of a huge battle (13-26 June) to drive out the Germans, after which it was developed as the main port for supplies to the Liberation forces. While that period robbed the town of its historic appearance, it has allowed Cherbourg to redevelop, modernize and remain a major port town.

Arriving in Cherbourg-Octeville

Getting there
There is a **bus station** ⓘ *Av Jean-François Millet, T02 33 44 32 22*. For details of regional bus services, see page 12. There is also a **train station** ⓘ *Av Jean-François Millet, T02 33 44 36 35*. For details of regional rail services, see page 11.

Getting around
Daytime public transport right across the city of Cherbourg-Octeville is provided by **Zéphir Bus** ⓘ *T08 10 81 00 50, zephirbus.com*, between about 0620 and 1945 Monday to Saturday, about 0750-1900 Sunday, additional limited service Friday and Saturday nights. Their website details routes, timetables and discount tickets. The central point for town buses is boulevard R Schumann where most lines intersect.

Tourist information
Office de Tourisme ⓘ *2 quai Alexandre III, T02 33 93 52 02, cherbourgtourisme.com, 15 Jun-15 Sep Mon-Sat 0930-1900, Sun 1000-1300, 1400-1700; 15 Sep-15 Jun Mon-Sat 1000-1230, 1400-1800, Sun (in school holidays only) 1000-1300*. Pick up the latest copy of *Le Mois* from shops or the tourist office to find out what's on this month in Cherbourg-Octeville.

Places to visit in Cherbourg-Octeville → *For listings, see pages 67-69.*

Parc Emmanuel Liais
ⓘ *Rond Point Leclerc, between rue de l'Abbaye and la rue de la Bucaille, T02 33 87 88 98. Open from about 0800 (0830 in winter) to 1700, 1830, 1930, depending on the month. Free.*
For a quiet stroll in the town centre, visit these public botanic gardens, bursting with 500 varieties of tropical plant, laid out in the 19th century.

Musée des Deaux Arts Thomas Henry (Thomas Henry Fine Arts Museum)
ⓘ *Reopens in 2015. 4 rue Vastel, T02 33 23 39 30.*
The town's most prestigious museum houses a notable art collection, with several works by Jean-François Millet, who grew up locally.

Cité de la Mer
ⓘ *Gare Maritime Transatlantique, T02 33 20 26 26, citedelamer.com. Open 0930 (1000 in winter)-1800, 1830 or 1900, with variations throughout the year, last tickets sold 1 hr before closing. Low season €15.50, €10.50 child (under 5s free), high season €18, €13 child (under 5s free).*
If you have some hours to pass in Cherbourg-Octeville, it's worth crossing to the right bank to visit this family attraction. There is a good aquarium here, said to be Europe's deepest, but the focus is on our relationship with the sea. The main attraction is an interesting self-guided tour of the nuclear submarine, *Redoubtable*. The Cité is located inside the former transatlantic station, next to the transatlantic dock, so with luck there may be a cruise liner moored alongside.

Fort de Roule – Musée de la Libération (Museum of the Liberation)
ⓘ *Fort du Roule, T02 33 20 14 12. May-Sep Tue-Sat 1000-1200 and 1400-1800, Sun afternoon only, Oct-Apr (except Dec-Jan – closed) Tue-Sun 1400-1800). €4, concessions €2.50.*

Also on the right bank, on a high ridge behind the harbour, the 19th-century Fort de Roule has a magnificent view over the town and its huge harbour. Inside the fortress, displays graphically record not simply the events of the liberation but also those that led to the defeat of France by the Nazis, and life during the German occupation. On display is an impressive collection of uniforms and weapons, maps of the period, scale models and photographs that bring the Liberation to life.

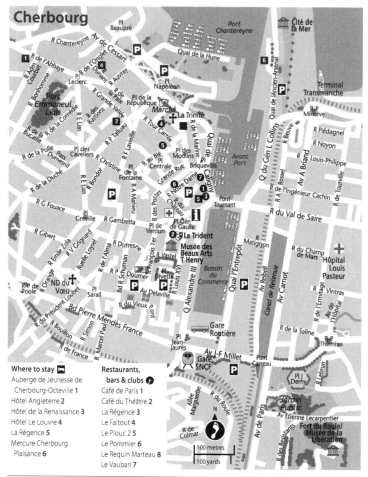

Cherbourg

Where to stay 🛏
Auberge de Jeunesse de
  Cherbourg-Octeville 1
Hôtel Angleterre 2
Hôtel de la Renaissance 3
Hôtel Le Louvre 4
La Régence 5
Mercure Cherbourg
  Plaisance 6

**Restaurants,
bars & clubs** 🍴
Café de Paris 1
Café du Théâtre 2
La Régence 3
Le Faitout 4
Le Plouc 2 5
Le Pommier 6
Le Requin Marteau 8
Le Vauban 7

Beaches
Cherbourg-Octeville has no proper beach, but during July and August there is a bus, Le Bus Plage, running from the city centre to the Plage de Collignon, just east of town, and Plage de Querqueville, to the west.

Cap de la Hague → *For listings, see pages 67-69.*

The most dramatic of the Cotentin's rugged coastal scenery lies west of Cherbourg-Octeville, in the area known as La Hague. Within moments, you are taken on narrow lanes from awesome sea cliffs to traditional small farms with stone farmhouses and muddy farmyards.

Take the main coast road out of Cherbourg-Octeville, heading west from place Napoléon along the D901 Just at the edge of town, at a roundabout where the road turns away from the sea, take D45, and follow it as it leaves Cherbourg-Octeville and its suburbs behind.

You will first approach Querqueville, where a hilltop chapel dating from the 10th century is one of the oldest churches in France. Skirt quiet Urville-Nacqueville, which has a good sandy beach and a beautiful 16th-century **château** ① *nacqueville.com, May-Sep Tue, Thu, Fri and Sun 1200-1700, €6,* standing in sheltered, wooded grounds (le Parc de Nacqueville) noted for its rhododendrons. The road climbs to the impressive towers and walls of 16th-century Dur-Ecu manor and arrives at the village of Landemer, with good sea views. Beyond it are magnificent roadside viewpoints. Just off to the right of D45, on D237, the seashore village of Gruchy was the birthplace of the artist François Millet (1814-1875), leading light of the Barbizon school. Child of a poor working family, he became a pioneer and one of the greatest proponents of painting natural scenes and ordinary working people. His former home (Maison Natale) can be visited on **guided tours** ① *Apr-Sep, and all school holidays (except Christmas), €4.20.*

Stay on D45 as it swings away from the seashore, eventually returning to it at little Omonville-la-Rogue, dominated by its solid, low 13th-century church. The village has a charming small harbour, edged with simple cottages. In the churchyard of its neighbour Omonville-la-Petite the poet Jacques Prévert (1900-1977) is buried. Port-Racine, just beyond, is another tiny and charming quayside village, and claims – quite plausibly – to be 'the smallest port In France'. The road now approaches the windy tip of Cap de la Hague, the far end of the peninsula, where several small communities cluster. The village of Goury, right on the cape, has an attractive harbour, and is renowned for the many lives saved by its brave lifeboat crew. The Goury lighthouse is well known to sailors in these capricious waters. At low tide, razor-edged rocks can be seen just beneath the waves. Goury's near-neighbour Auderville has two excellent 15th-century alabasters in an otherwise plain and simple 13th-century church.

D45 ends here. Much of the terrain on the south side of the cape feels wild and untouched. Follow steep, narrow D401 (or take the busier main road D901 across higher ground) to reach the turning on the left for Nez de Voidries and Nez de Jobourg, bird reserves and rocky headlands with high cliffs and glorious views to the Channel Islands. When you get back on to D901, turn right and hurry past a large nuclear reprocessing plant.

Steep lanes run between the main road and the sea. Take D318 from Beaumont-Hague down to Vauville, a delightful village of dry-stone walls and old stone houses. From here the D237 to Biville has magnificent coastal views. Biville is the home of a rather obscure cult, the veneration of Thomas Helye (1187-1257), known as *Le Bienheureux* (Blessed), a priest whose supposedly miracle-working remains are preserved in a modern shrine in the 13th-century church. A footpath (about 20 minutes each way) leads to a granite crucifix on a high point, known as the Calvaire des Dunes, from which there is a magnificent vista along the western Cotentin coast from Flamanville to Nez de Jobourg.

From Biville, climb D118 back to D901. Turn right for Cherbourg-Octeville. A turning on the right, rue du Bigard, leads up to the modern, family-oriented (but French only) **Ludiver Planétarium de la Hague** ① *T02 33 78 13 80, ludiver.com; site open Jul-Aug daily 1100-1830, rest of year Sun-Fri 1400-1800; planetarium shows Jul-Aug daily at 1130, 1500 and 1630, rest of year at 1500 only; €7.75, €5.60 child and concessions,* which has a museum about stars and planets, children's entertainment as well as the planetarium. D901 takes you the short distance back into Cherbourg-Octeville.

Cherbourg-Octeville listings

For hotel and restaurant price codes and other relevant information, see pages 13-17.

⊜ Where to stay

Cherbourg-Octeville *p62, map p64*
€€€-€€ Mercure Marine Hotel Cherbourg Plaisance, Allée du Président Menut, T02 33 44 01 11. In a very striking modern waterside building (with its latitude and longitude written across the front), standard rooms at this 3-star right-bank hotel may be considered a little short of the usual **Mercure** level, but the chief attraction here is proximity to the ferry terminal, just a few mins away. The pricier Superior rooms do provide decent comfortable accommodation, with harbour views. Free Wi-Fi. The hotel has a restaurant with familiar French fare, but the town centre is only about 10 mins' walk for better value.
€€ Hôtel Le Louvre, 2 rue Henri Dunant, T02 33 53 02 28, hotel-le-louvre-cherbourg. com. A decently comfortable, modern and efficiently run 2-star hotel about 15 mins' walk from the port and town centre, the Louvre is in a neighbourhood that can be a little noisy, but it has good soundproofing. Catering for both family holidays and business travellers, services and facilities are of a good standard and include Wi-Fi.
€€ La Régence, 42 quai Caligny, T02 33 43 05 16, laregence.com. This 3-star town centre family-run hotel on the quayside has simple, uncluttered, well equipped and tastefully decorated rooms. Service is friendly and efficient, and there's free Wi-Fi.
€ Auberge de Jeunesse de Cherbourg-Octeville, 55 rue de l'Abbaye, T02 33 78 15 15, fuaj.org/cherbourg-octeville. Reception 0800-1300 and 1800-2300, hostel open all year except Christmas and New Year. For low-budget accommodation in the city centre, the youth hostel is well placed in an attractively refurbished former French Navy building.

€ Hôtel Angleterre, 8 rue P Talluau, T02 33 53 70 06, hotelangleterre-fr.com. A modest, simple tourist hotel in solid corner premises in a quiet street, yet in the heart of the town, the Angleterre offers adequately equipped and inexpensive rooms.
€ Hôtel de La Renaissance, 4 rue de l'Eglise, T02 33 43 23 90, hotel-renaissance-cherbourg.com. Well placed in the city centre, this 2-star hotel offers clean, neat, rooms with views towards the port and the sea. No restaurant, but there are several nearby.

⊘ Restaurants

Cherbourg-Octeville *p62, map p64*
€€ Café de Paris, 40 quai Caligny, T02 33 43 12 36, restaurantcafedeparis.com. Mon 1900-2145, Tue-Sat 1200-1400 and 1900-2145, usually closed 2 weeks early in the year and 2 weeks in Nov. This popular and legendary fish and seafood restaurant was founded as long ago as 1803, but looks and feels modern. There are 3 dining rooms and outdoor tables too, and it could hardly be better placed, right on the main quayside.
€€ La Régence, 42 quai Caligny, T02 33 43 05 16, laregence.com. Daily 1200-1430 and 1930-2200. This is the restaurant of a traditional family-run hotel, attractive with awnings and flowers outside and a warm, rich Edwardian-style decor inside, with velvet and polished woods and partitions. It's very conveniently placed on the busy quayside near the bridge to the right bank and the car ferry. Service is friendly and efficient, with a choice of menus of French and Norman cooking, emphasising fresh shellfish.
€€ Le Faitout, 25 rue Tour Carrée, T02 33 04 25 04, restaurant-le-faitout.com. Mon-Sat lunch and dinner. In the main shopping area, this appealing, attractive and unpretentious bistro-style restaurant offers classic French fare, such as chicken liver terrine or salmon tart, at very reasonable prices.

€€ **Le Vauban**, 22 quai Caligny, T02 33 43
10 11. Tue-Fri 1200-1345 and 1900-2130,
Sat 1900-2130, Sun 1200-1400, closed
spring and autumn half-terms. A popular
and highly regarded bright modern
restaurant on the quayside, with a glass-
enclosed front section overlooking the
street. Excellent French cooking with the
emphasis on seafood.

€€-€ **Le Plouc 2**, 59 rue Blé, T02 33
01 06 46. Mon-Sun 1900-2130, Tue-Sat
1200-1400 and 1900-2130. Atmospheric
with old beams and tiles, much liked by
locals for straightforward menus of French
cooking skilfully and imaginatively prepared,
as well as generously and attractively
presented. Good wine list.

€ **Le Pommier**, 15 bis rue Notre Dame,
T02 33 53 54 60. Tue-Sat 1200-1400 and
1930-2230, closed 2 weeks in Jan, 3 weeks
in Nov. There's good value for money at this
bistro-style restaurant serving traditional
French dishes, such as pigeon in pastry.
Modern art hangs on the walls, and there
are periodic temporary exhibitions.

🌙 Bars and clubs

Cherbourg-Octeville *p62, map p64*
Café du Théâtre, 8 place Général de Gaulle,
T02 33 43 01 49, lecafedutheatre.com.
Tue-Sat 1000-2300 (0100 at weekends).
Once part of the ornate, Italianate theatre
which is right in front of it, this is now a
lively ground floor bar and upstairs brasserie,
ideal for drinks and people-watching before
or after a show. If you're hungry, there's a
choice of inexpensive dishes.
Le Requin Marteau, 20 rue de la Paix,
T02 33 53 15 74. Thu-Sat evenings.The
most popular dance disco with the young
Cherbourgeois. It is sometimes overcrowded
and often busy in the early hours of Sat
night and Sun morning. It's right in the city
centre, close to place Napoléon.

🎭 Entertainment

Cherbourg-Octeville *p62, map p64*
Casinos
Casino de Cherbourg, 18 quai Alexandre III,
T02 33 20 53 35. Daily 1030-0400 (0500
at weekends), daytime bar opens 1200,
nightclub Fri-Sat 2200-0500. Reputedly
the oldest casino in France, the building
itself was destroyed during the war, and its
successor completely refurbished in 2000.
Perhaps lacking the glamour of the original,
this is still a place to enjoy a dance, a dinner
and glitzy show and a roll of the dice – or
at least, of the slot machine. Enjoy a dinner
dance at its nightclub, **L'Amirauté**, or cross
the road to the casino's diner, themed as
1950s Americana and appropriately named
Fiftys Diner.

Circus arts
La Brèche, rue de la Chasse Verte, T02 33
88 43 73, labreche.fr. This "national centre
for circus arts" has greatly expanded in
recent years, making the city a focal point
for communication and cooperation
between circus entertainers. It also
hosts innovative circus-style shows
and perfomances throughout the year.

Music
Le Trident, Scène Nationale de Cherbourg-
Octeville (Trident National Stage), Place
du Général de Gaulle, T02 33 88 55 50,
trident-scenenationale.com. Cherbourg's
remarkable 19th-century 600-seat theatre,
built in an Italian style of ornate opulence
(and today known as the Théâtre à
l'Italienne), is the grandest of the 3 venues
used by the Trident combined stage
companies of Cherbourg-Octeville for
an interesting programme of arts and
entertainment including modern and
classical dance and music. The 2 other
venues are the 400-seat Théâtre de la Butte
and 240-seat Le Vox, the latter often hosting
innovative modern dance, drama and music.

O Shopping

Cherbourg-Octeville *p62, map p64*
Antiques and second-hand
Flea market, Place des Moulins, place de
la Révolution, rue d'Espagne and Parvis de
la Basilique Ste Trinité. 1st Sat of the month,
0800-1800. There are regular produce
markets every day of the week (except Mon)
in Cherbourg-Octeville and throughout
the region. Once a month comes the much
bigger **Marché aux Puces** (flea market)
filling Cherbourg-Octeville's central squares
with a variety of bric-à-brac, household
goods and clothing ranging from fine
antiques to junk.

O What to do

Cherbourg-Octeville *p62, map p64*
Guided tours
Cherbourg-Octeville guided walking
tours, 2 quai Alexandre III, T02 33 93 52 02,

cherbourgtourisme.com. Cherbourg-
Octeville tourist office run guided walking
tours visiting the sights of the town on
Sun afternoons, except in Jul and Aug
when tours are more frequent. The tours
are free, and leave from the tourist office
at 1430. Contact the tourist office (see
page 63) for information.

O Directory

Cherbourg-Octeville *p62, map p64*
Hospital Centre Hospitalier Public du
Cotentin, 46 rue du Val de Saire, T02 33 20
70 00, ch-cotentin.fr. **Pharmacy** There
are many pharmacies in the town centre,
including: Pharmacie Goffin, 1 place Général
de Gaulle, T02 33 20 41 29, and Pharmacie
Lepetit-Dupas, 49 rue Foch, T02 33 43 13 42.

Northern Cotentin

At first sight, the northern (or upper) Cotentin seems dominated by the modern industrial port town of Cherbourg-Octeville at its tip. Yet this part of the peninsula also preserves the greatest sense of unharnessed and unspoiled nature. It was here that the first Norse invaders set foot in Normandy, and here that they clung on longest to their old culture. Many village names incorporate a *bec* (stream, in Norse), *tot* (house) or *hougue* (low hill). Rocky headlands, panoramic sea views and enchanting little fishing harbours characterize the wild Cap de la Hague area, west of Cherbourg-Octeville. The temptation to get out of the car and have a good walk is irresistible! Everywhere, the sea feels close. The highlight is the lofty Nez de Jobourg cliffs facing towards the Channel Islands across the dangerous currents of the Alderney Races. East of Cherbourg-Octeville lies the more sheltered Val de Saire, where the little Saire river running through tranquil, rustic countryside. Barfleur and St-Vaast-la-Hougue are fishing ports with charming, old-fashioned quaysides and good little hotels and seafood restaurants. For a surprising contrast, head away from the coasts into the lanes and villages of the interior, a gentle, quiet landscape of streams and wildflower meadows, fields and woods of beech and oak.

Barfleur → *For listings, see pages 74-76.*

There's a long history behind the delightful scene of Barfleur's bustling fishing harbour, with its cobbled quaysides and simple stone houses looking on to the working trawlers and the dockside activity. It used to make a popular weekend outing for the residents of Cherbourg, but today is relatively little visited.

It was once a much larger town and more important harbour. In 1066 William the Conqueror's ship set sail from here on his campaign against England (William himself boarded it at Dives, on the coast near Caen), and it was from Barfleur that Richard the Lionheart set sail to England in 1194 to be crowned king. In 1120 the *Blanc Nef* foundered on the rocks off Pointe de Barfleur, just north of the town, with the loss of some three hundred members of the Anglo-Norman nobility – among them the heir to the English throne, William, son of Henry I.

Phare de Gatteville
① *25c la Route du Phare, Gatteville-le-Phare, T02 33 23 17 97, pharedegatteville.com. Daily 1000-1200 and 1400-closing time (as follows: Feb, part of Nov, Christmas: 1600; Mar, Oct: 1700; Apr, Sep: 1800; May-Aug: 1900), closed in bad weather, about €2.50, children free.*
Today, a seashore path takes you 4 km to the huge Gatteville Lighthouse, which now casts its warning from that treacherous headland. Almost 75 m tall, with 365 steps to the top, on a clear day the lighthouse gives a view reaching 30 km out to sea.

St-Vaast-la-Hougue → *For listings, see pages 74-76.*

With a name clearly revealing its Norse origins, St-Vaast is famous in France for its crabs and other shellfish and especially its high-quality oysters. Along the quayside, fishing boats are moored and lobster pots stacked high as fishermen sit fixing the snags in their nets, while scores of small yachts jostle at floating pontoons. The quayside leads round to a long jetty projecting into the waves and protecting the harbour. Such a large and deep harbour – and fortified, too – is far more than the fishermen or even the yachtsmen need. Those features date from past centuries, when St-Vaast was a bigger town, and much involved in wars between France and England. In a crucial episode, England's Catholic King James II, displaced by the Protestant William of Orange, massed a great Irish and French 'Catholic fleet' at St-Vaast in 1692. He intended to launch a great attack on England and regain his crown. But the Irish and French sailors would not work together and, coming under a surprise attack by an English and Dutch 'Protestant fleet', were routed before they had even set sail, in what was known as the Battle of La Hougue. There is a **information office** ① *place du Général de Gaulle, T02 33 23 19 32, saint-vaast-reville.com, Sep-Jun Tue-Sat 1000-1200, 1400-1800; Jul-Aug daily 1000-1230, 1400-1830.*

Ile de Tatihou
Just offshore is Tatihou Island (tatihou.com); fortified by Vauban, it is now inhabited mainly by a huge number of seabirds. Access to the island is limited to 500 visitors per day (to protect the wildlife; no dogs are allowed). The island is sometimes 'closed' to visitors in winter months.

Crossing to Tatihou At low tide, if the tidal coefficients are right, it's sometimes possible to get to the island on foot on a path called the Rhun that winds through the oysterbeds.

Allow 25 minutes for the walk. **Warning**: always check the tidal coefficients before crossing to Tatihou on foot. Even if the path appears to be safely uncovered, the coefficient must be 70 or more to allow sufficient time to cross safely there and back. The tourist office on the quayside can assist in case of uncertainty.

Or you can ride over to Tatihou from St-Vaast in a curious amphibious three-wheeled **ferry boat** ① *Quai Vauban, St-Vaast-la-Hougue, T02 33 23 19 92; Apr-Sep daily and Oct-Mar Sat-Sun, approximately 1000-1730 every 30-60 mins, timings according to the tide, 10-min trip; return €8.60, €3.50 child, under 4s free, includes entry to the Tour Vauban fort and museum on the island; return crossing only, €5.10, €2.30 child, one-way €3.50, €2 child.*

It was on Tatihou that King Edward II landed in 1346 to place his feet on French soil and claim the throne of France.

On the island, there are gardens, old shipwrights' workshops and a modest maritime heritage museum as well as **Vauban's fort** or tower ① *Apr-mid Oct daily 1000-1800. Otherwise, when open, afternoons only. Entry to the fort and museum may be paid for as part of the ferry fare to the island, or purchased separately if preferred from Accueil Tatihou on quai Vauban in St-Vaast.* The 21-m-tall tower, declared a World Heritage Site in 2008, contains a gunpowder store, sleeping quarters and canon platform, and has its own fortified farm.

The high point of Tatihou's year is the folk-rock festival **Festival des Traversées Tatihou**, held there every August, with plenty of events also held on the St-Vaast quayside. It is possible to stay on the island in simple lodgings (see page 74).

St-Mère-Eglise → *For listings, see pages 74-76.*

This village lies just inland from Utah Beach (see page 57). German soldiers marched into Ste-Mère on 18 June 1940 and established Nazi rule here, as everywhere in the Cotentin. Almost four years later, in the evening of 5 June 1944, the sky over the village was filled by 811 US Air Force planes, which dropped 14,238 parachutists of the 82nd and 101st airborne divisions on to Ste-Mère. The Americans took control of the village just before midnight.

Eglise
① *Place de l'Eglise. Daily, about 0800-1800.*
Famously, during the night of 5 June 1944 one wretched American parachutist got caught on the church tower and hung there for hours – an incident shown in the film *The Longest Day*. A dummy representing him, his billowing parachute caught above, remains there to this day and is still a shocking and pitiful image. Inside the church, the oldest parts of which date from the 11th century, a vivid modern stained-glass window depicts the Virgin Mary surrounded by parachutists and planes. A second window is a gift from US parachute regiment veterans. You'll see other memorials of the Liberation around the church square.

Musée Airborne
① *14 rue Eisenhower, T02 33 41 41 35, musee-airborne.com. Apr-Sep 0900-1845, Feb-Mar and Oct-Dec 1000-1700, €7, €4 child, veterans free.*
Just across the square from the church, the town's museum is in two buildings, one under a roof representing a landing parachute and the other representing the wing of a plane. Displays range from a genuine Douglas C47 plane and WACO glider to uniforms, vehicles, weapons and evocative documents and photographs.

Barneville and Carteret → *For listings, see pages 74-76.*

Barneville and Carteret (barneville-carteret.fr) are neighbouring small towns that have joined together administratively, yet preserve quite distinct and separate characters. Between them lies a large natural harbour in the estuary of the River Gerfleur. From the harbour, you can catch a ferry to Jersey. It's close enough for a day trip. On the south side of the Gerfleur, set back from the harbour, quiet Barneville is mainly residential. At its heart is an 11th-century church and there's a good street market on Saturdays with masses of fresh fish and shellfish. Between the harbour and the sandy seashore, Barneville's rather sedate but very popular well-equipped modern family beach resort is called Barneville-Plage.

On the north side of the harbour is the livelier and more atmospheric small fishing town of Carteret. There's a sandy beach on this side too, smaller but well sheltered. It leads out towards a rocky cape called Cap de Carteret, last of the Cotentin headlands before the tamer coasts of Southern Cotentin. On the cliff top stand a chapel and a lighthouse.

At low tide, miles of sand and rock pools along the Barneville-Carteret waterfronts are exposed. You can find a huge selection of shellfish, especially crabs and shrimps.

Lessay → *For listings, see pages 74-76.*

In what was then an open and uninhabited part of the Cotentin – today it is lightly wooded farming country – 1000 years ago the quiet village of Lessay grew around a lonely abbey. The Benedictine community built a fine **abbey church** ① *usually open daily 0900-1800, except during services,* here in 1050. It later years it was altered, and for centuries was considered one of the loveliest examples of Norman Romanesque architecture and a pioneer in its development of the style. During the bombardment of 1944, the church was very badly damaged, but was skilfully repaired by stonemasons from 1945 to 1958. Sturdy, plain and unadorned, it is quiet, restful, perfectly symmetrical and pleasingly proportioned. The masons used the same elegant pale stone as before, although the older stone appears to have a slightly pinker tint. The church contains a modern organ, installed in 1994, and is a delightful place to enjoy classical concerts during July and August.

Northern Cotentin listings

For hotel and restaurant price codes and other relevant information, see pages 13-17.

◗ Where to stay

Barfleur *p71*

€€ Conquérant, 16-18 rue St-Thomas-à-Becket, T02 33 54 00 82, hotel-leconquerant.com. Closed mid-Nov to end Mar. In an appealing 17th-century stone building close to the port, this traditional 2-star hotel has simple, pleasing rooms, all very varied, most with a view into the lovely garden. Breakfast is served, and in the evening dinner with savoury and sweet crêpes.

Carneville

€ Les Deux Caps, 2 La Brasserie, T02 33 54 13 81, gitedesdeuxcaps.com. Exceptionally good value, this high-quality B&B is close to Cap Lévy, 12 km from Cherbourg, in delightful Val de Saire countryside with a spacious garden and views towards the sea (it's about 2.5 km from beaches). The house is attractively decorated and furnished with rustic touches. Rooms are comfortable and simple, with calm, pale colours. The owner is a former chef who has worked in Michelin-starred restaurants. She serves an excellent *table d'hôte* (set dinner) for an additional €23 per person, drinks included.

St-Vaast-la-Hougue *p71*

€€-€ France-et-Fuchsias, 20 rue Marechal, T02 33 54 40 41, france-fuchsias.com. Closed some weeks during the winter. This satisfyingly traditional place, set back from the street behind a cobbled courtyard and gorgeously draped in fuchsias, is a delightful little hotel of charm and character. Steep, narrow stairs climb to simple, pleasant rooms, with wicker furniture. There's a strong fuchsia theme throughout, with fuchsia-coloured carpet, wallpaper, picture frames and lampshades. It's noted too for its excellent seafood restaurant;

strictly speaking, the France is the hotel, and the Fuchsias the restaurant, but both are known as France-et-Fuchsias. It's just a few paces from St-Vaast's bustling, picturesque quayside. Outstanding value.

Ile de Tatihou *p71*

€ Tatihou Island, T02 33 54 33 33, tatihou.com. Contact in advance to check availability. In the island's sturdy granite buildings there is simple accommodation of single, double and triple rooms with en suite facilities. Enjoy nature, peace, the sea and the stars. Prices are €85 for full-board (€41 child) or €62 half-board (€32 child). There is no room-only rate.

Carteret *p73*

€€€ Marine, 11 rue de Paris, T02 33 53 83 31, hotelmarine.com. Mar-23 Dec. With a bright beachy atmosphere and a seafront terrace in the heart of the resort, this small 19th-century hotel (run by the same family since opening) has comfortable, light and airy bedrooms and one of the best restaurants in the département.

€€€ Ormes, Promenade Barbey-d'Aurevilly, T02 33 52 23 50, hoteldesormes.fr. Closed for a month Jan-Feb. A solid and comfortable, ivy-draped boutique hotel (12 rooms), exquisitely decorated in warm soothing pale tones contrasting with white, and furnished in the best home-from-home style (if only one's home could be as nice as this!). Outside there's a lovely garden terrace and harbour views. The hotel also has a good restaurant.

◉ Restaurants

Barfleur *p71*

€ Le Moderne, 1 place de Gaulle, T02 33 23 12 44. Closed Jan to mid-Feb. This attractive building with terrace in front is a good-value country restaurant, with slightly fussy decor and sometimes chilly, indifferent service, but well-prepared menus. The speciality is local fish and seafood, especially oysters, but there's a wide range of other French and Norman dishes.

St-Vaast-la-Hougue p71
€€ France-et-Fuchsias, 20 rue Marechal, T02 33 54 40 41, france-fuchsias.com. Lunch and dinner, closed some weeks during the winter. In St-Vaast's quiet 'main street' a few mins' walk from its attractive fishing harbour, this enticing restaurant (more correctly just called Les Fuchsias, while its hotel is La France) is draped in the foliage and flowers of a huge climbing fuchsia. Inside, the decor and menus are tasteful and traditional, but high quality. Fresh seafood is very much the speciality, but there are plenty of other dishes too. Sample mackerel stuffed with leeks, and sea bream with cream of cauliflower, broad beans, peas and chorizo. Many of the ingredients come from their own farm, close by.

Carteret p73
€€€ Restaurant de la Marine, 11 rue de Paris, T02 33 53 83 31, hotelmarine.com. Mid-Mar-11 Nov, contact for opening hours. Eat in the light and airy dining room with sea views, or get even closer to the view on the terrace, at this Michelin-starred restaurant noted for imaginative, beautifully presented French and Norman cooking.
€€ Le Rivage, Promenade Barbey-d'Aurevilly, T02 33 52 23 50, hoteldesormes. fr. Tue-Fri 1900-2130, Sat-Sun 1200-1400, 1900-2130, closed for a month Jan-Feb. In the elegant, charming Hôtel des Ormes, draped with the foliage of an climbing plant, this is a place to sample local lamb and the freshest fish and seafood, beautifully cooked and presented. At lunchtime, eat out of doors and enjoy sea views.

❀ Festivals

Ile Tatihou p71
Les Traversées Tatihou, on Tatihou island and St-Vaast-la-Hougue waterfront, T02 33 05 95 88, book at Accueil Tatihou, quai Vauban, Saint-Vaast-la-Hougue, or online by following the link at http://tatihou. manche.fr/festival-traversees-tatihou.asp. 4 days usually on the 3rd weekend in Aug. Tatihou's festival of folk music, with the emphasis on Celtic and traditional music and seafaring culture. There is a special atmosphere thanks to the remote and enchanting setting, and the crossing to the island, which many festival-goers do in bare feet. Performance times have to be arranged according to the tide, though there are also late-night festival events at St-Vaast on the quayside and in the bars.

Lessay p73
La Foire de Ste-Croix (Holy Cross Fair), 3-4 days every Sep on the 2nd weekend. On these end-of-summer days, Lessay hosts one of Normandy's biggest, liveliest and oldest country fairs. The main activity is the trading of cattle, horses and other animals. Lamb is grilled throughout the fair. Les Heures Musicales de l'Abbaye de Lessay, Eglise Abbatiale de Lessay, bookings via Lessay tourist office, 11 place St Cloud, Lessay, T02 33 45 14 34, canton-lessay.com. Latest details at http://lesheuresmuses. blogspot.com. The beautiful Romanesque abbey and its convent buildings provide the setting for this annual programme of concerts of classical music and choral performances for about 6 weeks during Jul and Aug.

◎ Shopping

St-Vaast-la-Hougue p71
Food and drink
Maison Gosselin, 27 rue de Verüe, T02 33 54 40 06, maison-gosselin.fr. Tue-Fri 0900-1230 and 1430-1900, Sat 0900-1230, 1500-1930,

Sun 0900-1230, Mon closed (except in summer, 0930-1230, 1500-1900). One of the highlights of a visit to St-Vaast-la-Hougue is to look in at this legendary *épicerie*. Opened in 1889 by Clovis Gosselin, it has remained in the family ever since. With a gleaming red façade, it's now run by Clovis' great-granddaughter Françoise and her husband Bertrand. Along with a vast array of ordinary products, its shelves are loaded with the finest Normandy cheeses and their own wide range of top-quality home-made pâtés and terrines (for example, pork pâté mixed with Livarot cheese), tripes à la mode de Caen, conserves and confectionery. In addition to such edible treats, the shop also stocks unusual souvenirs and children's toys, such as dolls' house furniture.

Southern Cotentin

Inland, especially in its southern half, the Cotentin peninsula broadens out into the varied and attractive small-scale farming country called *bocage*. The sea feels further away and less dominant. The land becomes gentler. Sunken lanes weave between tall hedges and orchards and fields of good rich pasture. Several of the thriving little country towns have a long history – this was a centre of pre-Roman civilization, then of Roman rule and was populous in the Middle Ages too. Along its west coast, the Manche *département* intersperses sandy beaches and dunes, marshes where seabirds cluster, small harbour towns and rocky headlands. Here and there are remnants of German gun emplacements. There's a string of little holiday resorts, including Portbail, with its Romanesque church and Gallo-Roman baptistry, and Coutainville, with superb beach and fin-de-siècle charm. Granville is altogether bigger and busier, with plenty of interest in its Upper and Lower towns. The coast road south of town curves along the Bay of Mont-St-Michel at the foot of the Cotentin Peninsula, giving some exquisite views.

Occupying a hilltop position, this appealing and attractive small cathedral city has existed here in one form or another for at least 2000 years. Under the name Cosedia, it was the main settlement of the Unelli tribe whose resistance to Roman rule proved troublesome to Caesar. Eventually subdued by Rome in 56 BC, it had to be defended during the Roman occupation. By about AD 500, Coutances became the seat of an important bishopric whose authority included the Channel Islands, and had a cathedral. Ninth-century Viking raiders almost destroyed the town and drove away the clergy and the rest of population, but rebuilt a Norse town of their own among the ruins, complete with a new cathedral in their Norman Romanesque style. In 1218, Coutances was damaged again, by fire, which is why its present cathedral dates from that time. Bombed in 1944, the town has once more recovered and much of it has been restored, although the loss of many buildings is plain to see.

Cathédrale de Notre-Dame de Coutances

ⓘ *Rue Tancrède, cathedralecoutances.free.fr. Daily 0900-1900 (1800 in winter). Free; extensive programme of guided tours available, ask at tourist office.*

Luckily, Coutances' greatest possession survived the war. The cathedral stands on the main street at the summit of the town. Its three tall towers are visible from afar, one of them a massive octagonal lantern tower soaring to 41 m. Beautiful inside and out, Coutances cathedral is numbered among the great masterpieces of Norman Gothic architecture. Yet curiously, although built in the 13th century, it was constructed closely around the framework of its 11th-century Romanesque predecessor, parts of the building being Gothic stonework attached to the Romanesque structure.

The total effect is of elegant simplicity and masterful workmanship, bringing together solidity and finesse. Inside, arches are high and narrow, the aisles open on to a succession of side chapels, and the inside of the lantern tower is surprisingly beautiful. Some of the sculpture and the rich blue stained glass on the west front dates right back to its 13th-century reconsecration. There is plenty of later work, too, including the very striking and graceful Notre-Dame de la Circata, a 14th-century marble sculpture of a colourfully draped Madonna and Child depicted as essentially just an ordinary, wistful mother (albeit wearing a crown) holding her little boy on her arm. This touching image, standing in the painted Lady Chapel, attracted large numbers of pilgrims during the turmoil of the Hundred Years War.

The much-revered Chapelle Religeuse displays a remarkable collection of body parts and bodily fragments, supposedly being the relics of numerous important saints, bishops, abbots, priests, martyrs and other Catholic celebrities, as well as pieces of the Cross and even the crown of thorns.

Most medieval stained-glass windows tell a story, often from the Bible or the lives of saints. Look closely at the stained glass in the north transept of the cathedral and you'll see that it tells the story of Thomas à Becket, who was murdered in Canterbury cathedral in 1170.

Jardin des Plantes

ⓘ *Rue Quesnel-Morinière, T02 33 19 08 10. Daily 0900-1700 (except Jul-Aug, open to 2300 with illuminations). Free.*

The square in front of the cathedral is the town's marketplace, and just a few minutes' walk on the other side of it is the entrance of the extensive 19th-century Jardin des Plantes.

This delightful green park has wonderfully imaginative herbaceous displays, lawns, copses and narrow, flowery paved terraces with fountains. In summer, illuminations and music make it quite magical. At the entrance to the gardens, **Musée Quesnel-Morinière** ① *2 rue Quesnel Morinière, T02 33 07 07 88, Mon and Wed-Sat 1000-1200 and 1400-1700 (Jul Aug 1800), Sun 1400-1700, €2.50, children free*, displays a variety of local arts and traditional regional craftsmanship, and there are some good paintings too, with some surprises – notably, a painting by Rubens of *Lions and Dogs Fighting*.

Granville → *For listings, see pages 81-83.*

Larger than the other Cotentin beach resorts, Granville attracts summer crowds, and has done for more than a century. It's divided into the sombre fortified Upper Town (Ville Haute), high on a rocky ridge rising sheer from the sea, and the newer Lower Town (Ville Basse). The Upper Town came into being as an English fort in the 15th century. They rapidly lost control of it, and in 1695 it was the English themselves who almost destroyed the town when they attacked *corsaires* (pirates) who were based here. Granville began to flourish again with the growth of its fishing harbour, which grew to become the Lower Town, and in the 19th century began its career as a holiday resort.

Cross the drawbridge and pass through the Grande Porte, a 16th-century gatehouse, into the Upper Town. Just inside the gate, the **Musée du Vieux Granville** ① *2 rue Lecarpentier, T02 33 50 44 10, Apr-Sep Wed-Mon 1000-1200 and 1400-1800 (1830 in Jul-Aug), Oct-Dec and Feb-Mar Wed, Sat and Sun 1400-1800, €1.75, €1 concessions and under 11s free*, gives background information about the town that proves useful when you are strolling around. Turn right along quiet, narrow and atmospheric old streets of granite 18th-century houses to reach the large and airy main square, Place de l'Isthme. The square gives spectacular sea views. From here, the Iles Chausey, 16 km away, seem very close. Further away, the hills of Brittany rise from the horizon. If you're tempted to visit the Chausey Islands, which are administratively part of Granville, you can catch a ferry there from the harbour in the bustling and lively Lower Town, where the animated marina is the focal point.

Musée d'Art Moderne Richard Anacréon
① *Place de l'Isthme, T02 33 51 02 94. May-Sep Tue-Wed 1100-1800, Oct-Apr Wed-Sun 1400-1800. €2.70, €1.10 concessions, under 10s free, fees liable to alteration, temporary exhibitions may have their own opening hours and entry fees.*
The art museum in the Upper Town's main square came into being when a private collector gave Granville his whole collection of 280 works of art and 550 annotated books, forming an unrivalled assembly of modern late 19th and 20th-century art and literature. Painters in the collection include Derain, van Dongen, Vlaminck, Utrillo, Laurencin, Signac, Friesz, Cross and Luce. Among the books and manuscripts are extraordinary rare volumes and first editions, by such authors as Apollinaire, Cocteau, Colette, Genet, Loti and Valéry. The museum hosts a succession of prestigious temporary exhibitions.

Musée Christian Dior
① *Villa Les Rhumbs, rue Estouteville, T02 33 61 48 21, musee-dior-granville.com. Dates variable (depending on exhibitions) but generally 1 May-20 Sep, daily 1000-1830; in winter, school holidays and weekends, afternoons only. €4, €3 concessions, under 12s.*
Overlooking the sea from the north side of the Lower Town, the museum occupies the childhood home of the great *couturier*. A grand 1920s private house, it exhibits a

dazzling collection of Dior's work as well as personal memorabilia. Every year there's an all-summer special exhibition. The park-like garden, too, with lawns, trees and colourful flowerbeds, is very beautiful, especially the rose garden. There's also an elegant *salon de thé*, with tables on the lawn.

Iles Chausey (Chausey Islands) → For listings, see pages 81-83.

The Chausey Islands have an exceptionally large tidal range, with 14 m difference between low and high tide. At low tide, hundreds of rocks and small islands are revealed. The largest of the 50 islands that are still visible when the tide comes back in, and the only one inhabited, Grande Ile de Chausey has a permanent population said to number fewer than 10 people, but in summer scores of visitors, fishermen and sailing enthusiasts spend time in this away-from-it-all haven. It's fascinating to walk the paths of Grande Ile and explore the simple watery world of these granite islands. The Chausey Islands are the only Channel Islands under the control of France. All the Channel Islands remained a possession of the Dukes of Normandy after the French crown abolished the Duchy in 1469 and in 1500 the Chausey Islands were abandoned by the Channel Islands government based in Jersey and were granted to France.

Though apparently just low-lying fragments of rock when seen from a distance, when one steps ashore on to Grande Ile de Chausey it is transformed into a spacious, airy, green landscape of stony hills, dunes and heathland, wild flowers and seabirds. There's a church and cottages, a hamlet called Les Blainvillais and cultivated fields and gardens. Two old forts stand guard, 16th-century at one end of the island, 19th-century at the other. There's also a hotel and restaurant.

Southern Cotentin listings

For hotel and restaurant price codes and other relevant information, see pages 13-17.

○ Where to stay

Coutances *p78*

€€ Cositel, Rue St-Malo, T02 33 19 15 00, cositel.fr. The twee name conceals a comfortable low-budget modern hotel, with simple neat decor and bright uncluttered interiors all adding up to something perhaps better than its 2-star rating suggests. There's free broadband internet access in all bedrooms and the hotel also has its own restaurant serving modern French cooking, artfully presented.

€ Taverne du Parvis, Place Parvis Notre Dame, T02 33 45 13 55, hotelleparvi free fr Facing the front of Coutances cathedral, this traditional old hotel-restaurant-brasserie has a dozen simple 1-star rooms with shower and TV, at very inexpensive prices. Especially good value is the overnight half-board (dinner, bed and breakfast), Mon-Thu only.

Chambres d'hôtes

€€ Le Mascaret, 1 rue de Bas, Blainville sur mer, T02 33 45 86 09, restaurant-lemascaret. fr. Closed most of Jan and 10 days in Nov. Off the beaten track, by the sea near Coutances, this is a guesthouse with a difference. Instead of the usual home-from-home feel, here is a luxurious haven, an 18th-century house, courtyard and garden, with interesting, elegant rooms and suites, some decorated with Baroque exoticism, as well as pampering spa treatments, excellent breakfasts and, to cap it all, a Michelin-starred restaurant!

Granville *p79*

€€€-€€ Mercure Le Grand Large, 5 rue Falaise, T02 33 91 19 19, mercure-granville. com. With an appealing decor of pale woods and rugs, and a bright maritime feel on balconies and terraces, this comfortable, modern little resort hotel well deserves its 3 stars. It stands in a lofty position by the sea (there's a steep climb to reach it), overlooking the beach in one direction, the rooftops of the town centre in the other. It also has a good spa with seawater treatments.

€€-€ Bains, 19 rue Clemenceau, T02 33 50 17 31, hoteldesbains-granville.com. Closed most of Jan. By the waterfront just below the old town, at one end of the beach, the hotel is part of the 1920s complex that includes Granville's casino. Pleasantly decorated in pale tones, rooms are modest and rather variable, but some are attractive, with sea views and jacuzzi.

Iles Chausey (Chausey Islands) *p80*

€€€ Fort et Iles, Grande Ile de Chausey, T02 33 50 25 02, hotel chausey.com. Mid-Apr to end Sep. Prices are for half-board – there is no room-only or B&B option. Look not for creature comforts but for peace and quiet and even a touch of romance about the location when the day-trippers have departed. Chausey's simple, old-fashioned little hotel (just 8 rooms, 4 with sea views) offers utter tranquillity. Rooms are small, have no televisions, and are expensive, and service arguably lacks polish, but the white-washed maritime freshness of the decor and the garden setting have a good deal of charm.

Gîtes

€ Iles Chausey Gîtes Communaux, Ancien Presbytère, Grande Ile de Chausey, T02 33 91 30 03, ville-granville.fr/iles_chausey_ pratique.asp. Apr-Sep: minimum stay 1 week. Oct-Mar: shorter stays possible. May be closed part of the winter. The former school and rectory building close to the old fort on Grande Ile are divided into 5 *gîtes* providing adequate accommodation that captures something of the flavour of island life. The *gîtes* can each accommodate from

🍴 Restaurants

Coutances p78

€€ **Le Mascaret**, 1 rue de Bas, Blainville sur Mer, T02 33 45 86 09, restaurant-lemascaret.fr. 1200-1345 daily except Mon; 1915-2100 daily except Sun and Mon.
By the sea near Coutances, in an elegant, imaginative and luxurious setting, this highly inventive Michelin-starred restaurant brings together many influences to create delicious dishes in a relaxed, spontaneous style. Local carrots, for example, could appear as anything from crisps to ice-cream, while desserts may involve liquid nitrogen. The flagship menu promises to combine the arts, technology and tradition!

€ **Taverne du Parvis**, Place Parvis Notre Dame, T02 33 45 13 55, hotelleparvi.free.fr. Open all day. Facing the front of Coutances cathedral, this hotel-restaurant-brasserie has an old-fashioned pub-like appeal, with wooden façade, tiled floors, brass fittings and beer and cider on tap. Salads and snacks are on offer, as well as good-value set menus of classic French, Norman and Alsatian brasserie fare at modest prices, such as ham braised in cider, *choucroute* and *flammeküche*.

Granville p79

The oysters of Cotentin are acclaimed in France. Those produced on the stretch of Cotentin coastline from Granville to Portbail are especially renowned. Gourmets discern a distinctive 'flavour of the ocean' in these *pleine mer* (open seas) oysters, thanks to the clear waters and strong currents.

€€ **La Citadelle**, 34 rue du Port, T02 33 50 34 10, restaurant-la-citadelle.com. Thu-Tue 1200-1400, 1900-2130. Closed for about a month Dec-Jan. Enjoy attractively presented fresh fish, local lobster and other seafood, as well as other French and Norman dishes, in a restaurant whose light, fresh decor of blue and white with pale wood gives a distinctly nautical feel. There's an enclosed outdoor terrace at the front.

Cafés

Salon de Thé – Musée Christian Dior, Musée Christian Dior, rue Estouteville, T02 33 61 48 21. Jul-Aug daily 1100-1830. At this elegant villa where haute-couturier Christian Dior spent his childhood, and which is now a museum devoted to him, there's a delightful *salon de thé* with tables on the lawn and views of the sea.

Iles Chausey (Chausey Islands) p80

€€ **Hôtel du Fort et des Iles**, Grande Ile de Chausey, T02 33 50 25 02, hotel-chausey.com. Mid-Apr to Sep Tue-Sun lunch and dinner (open Mon on national holidays). Jolly and informal, with 2 rooms and an outdoor dining area with wonderful sea views, the restaurant offers limited set menus naturally strongly focused on fish and especially the Chausey islands' renowned lobster and other ocean-fresh shellfish.

✵ Festivals

Granville p79

Festival des Coquillages et des Crustacés, early Oct. A cornucopia of crustaceans are dished up at this jolly gourmet extravaganza in France's leading shellfish port. Vast quantities are sold ready-to-eat and consumed on the spot, and there are also stalls where you can learn how to cook, open and eat them.

Granville Carnival, weekend before Mardi Gras (Shrove Tuesday). Ancient traditions of a seafaring community live on in these 4 days of parades, music and festivities under the rule of a Carnival King.

🛍 Shopping

Villedieu-les-Poêles

For an interesting shopping excursion, travel 30 km inland from Granville to the

(continued) 4-7 people. Bookings must be made through the Office de Tourisme in Granville.

strangely named town of Villedieu-les-Poêles ("God's Town of Pans"), which has a 1000-year tradition of making high-quality copper kitchenware.

Walk along the central place de la République and rue Carnot and the side streets to find many small shops selling these classic cooking pots and pans.

Villedieu has also been an important market town for centuries.

Its weekly Grand Marché is still one of the biggest markets in the Manche *département* (every Tue morning, in place des Halles, place des Costils, place de la République and place du Presbytère). It's divided into sections, each in their own square, but the emphasis is firmly on local Normandy produce, with sellers of sausages, crème fraîche and butter, eggs and hens, fresh fish, home-made preserves and much more, including on-the-spot cooking of favourite snacks and takeaway fare.

⊙ What to do

Granville *p79*
Golf
Granville Golf Club, Bréville-sur-Mer, T02 33 50 23 06, www.golfdegranville.com. This excellent course, 5991 m long, combines an 18-hole course and a 9-hole which meander through natural dunes and undulating fairways close to the sea just north of Granville.

Tours
Granville Office de Tourisme, Cours Jonville, Granville, T02 33 91 30 03, granville-tourisme.fr. €3, under 12s free, evening tour of Christian Dior gardens free. Granville tourist office provides several themed guided tours (in French only) to enable visitors to discover the cultural heritage and maritime history of the town. All start at 1500 at the tourist office and last about 1½ hrs, except the unusual and enjoyable evening visit to the gardens at the Musée Christian Dior, which is free and starts at the entrance to the gardens.

Le Mont-St-Michel

Its setting in a vast space of sky and shore and water, and the remembrance of a time when the pious risked their lives crossing these treacherous sands and marshes on foot, and indeed the very idea of trying to build an abbey at the summit of this islet of granite, all contribute to the sense of wonder on seeing Le Mont-St-Michel. For religious and secular alike, it's an evocative, compelling sight, whether on a clear spring morning or in autumn mist, on a sunny afternoon or by moonlight, in the romantic mood of its nightly illuminations, or most especially when a high tide rushes frighteningly across the flats, now safely crossed by a causeway. The island's daunting stone ramparts rise as if part of the natural rock of the island, and from within them the lofty walls and spires of the abbey church reach up, culminating in a single immensely tall black pinnacle, on the very point of which gilded St Michael is poised triumphant. At the foot of the abbey a tiny village of narrow streets and stairs, its Grand'Rue packed with souvenir shops and cafés and distractions, caters to huge numbers of tourists crowding their way to and from the narrow Grand Degré steps that lead into the abbey precincts.

Come in springtime, early in the morning, or late in the afternoon, to see Le Mont-St-Michel without tour-bus groups. Better still, stay overnight in one of the island's hotels.

Arriving in Le Mont-St-Michel

Getting there

Information about access to Le Mont-St-Michel is on the website accueilmontsaintmichel.fr. Arriving in the area by car, signs indicate the way to the site's car park, which is 2.5 km from Le Mont-St-Michel. On reaching the car park you will be directed to available parking spaces. The price of parking is €8.50 for a car (€2.50 from 1900-0200 only), €12.50 for a campervan or similar, €3.50 for a motorbike. Cars with a disabled badge have to pay, but are given places reserved for them if available. A free shuttle bus to Le Mont leaves from a stop 800 m from the car park. For rail travellers, the nearest station is Pontorson, from which a shuttle bus direct to Le Mont costs €2 each way.

Never be tempted to make the crossing to Le Mont-St-Michel on the sands at low tide, or even to take a short walk from Le Mont. When the tide turns, the sea races back over the flats at about 1 m per second. Victor Hugo described it coming in at "the speed of a galloping horse".

Getting around

Wear comfortable walking shoes and be prepared for a lot of exercise. The Grand Degré has 350 stairs, followed by several hundred more while visiting the abbey. The only part of Le Mont-St-Michel that can be accessed without climbing any stairs is Grand'Rue.

Orientation

From the causeway, walk through the fortified Porte de l'Avancée gateway that leads through the ramparts on to Grand'Rue, the main street of Le Mont-St-Michel.

Tourist information

The Tourist Information Centre ① *T02 33 60 14 30, ot-montsaintmichel.com*, at the car park provides toilets, baby-changing facilities, and kennels (€7; dogs are not allowed in the Abbey or on the shuttle buses) as well as information. There's a tourist office in the Corps de Garde des Bourgeois, a 16th-century guard house, just inside the gateway on to the island.

Abbaye de St-Michel → For listings, see page 88.

① *T02 33 89 80 00, mont-saint-michel.monuments-nationaux.fr. Daily, May-Aug 0900-1900, Sep-Apr 0930-1800, last admission 1 hr before closing. €9, concessions €5.50, EU citizens under 26 free, all under18s free, disabled free. There's no charge to enter the abbey if you are attending Mass. Times of services are shown on the community's website, abbaye-montsaintmichel.com. You can tour the abbey on your own or pay an extra €4.50 for an audioguide (or €6 for 2), which will lead you on a tour of about 1¼ hrs. Guided tours are possible only for pre-booked groups.*

From the Grand Degré steps, wider stairs lead to the Plate-forme du Saut Gautier (Gautier's Leap Terrace), which gives access to the Eglise Abbatiale (abbey church) and the maze of other abbey buildings. The abbey came into being in AD 708 after Bishop Aubert of nearby Avranches had visualized it standing on the rock which at that time was called Mont Tombe (another smaller outcrop to the north is still called Tombelaine). Within 150 years the abbey he founded was attracting pilgrims. In the 10th century it became a border outpost of the new Duchy of Normandy, and was heavily fortified by the Norsemen, who peopled it with a Benedictine community. The enlargement of the abbey and rebuilding in Romanesque style began.

During the wars between the Anglo-Normans and the French, the buildings had to be repaired and partly rebuilt and the ramparts enlarged. Le Mont and its abbey became not only an increasingly popular and prestigious pilgrimage centre, but also a powerful French garrison. At the same time, beautiful Gothic construction started to replace the crumbling Romanesque structures. Thirteenth-century additions on the north side, commissioned by the French monarch, still known as La Merveille (The Marvel), are on three levels, with two wings (east and west), attached to the Romanesque crypt at the bottom, and the church at the upper level. More fine Gothic work was added at the end of the 15th century.

In the 16th century, the abbey began a long decline, and by the time of the Revolution had all but ceased to function. The buildings were turned into a prison, and so remained until Victor Hugo led a campaign to rescue Le Mont-St-Michel for the nation. In 1874, having closed the prison, the French government set out to restore and enhance the abbey, in the process making many changes to its appearance, rebuilding much of Grand'Rue and creating the solid causeway. That process has continued right up to the present day. The cloister gardens were added as recently as the 1960s. A religious community took up residence in the abbey once again in 1966.

The exterior of the Eglise Abbatiale (Abbey church) is a triumph of exuberant Gothic craftsmanship. Inside, the church is spacious and combines the sturdy, simple elegance of the older Romanesque crypts and nave with a glorious later Gothic choir. From the nave, pass into the wonderfully graceful cloister with elegant twin arcades and enter the monks' vast refectory. You are now on the upper level of La Merveille. Provisions were brought to the upper level using the great wheel, a huge pulley operated by a treadmill. On lower levels, the knights' hall and guests' hall are awesome spaces supported by rows of columns. On a guided group tour, you may visit the older crypts that support the abbey buildings, including the most ancient and affecting, Notre-Dame-Sous-Terre (Our Lady Below Ground).

A multimedia show, **Archéoscope** ① *Grand'Rue, Le Mont-St-Michel, T02 33 89 01 85, archeoscope-montsaintmichel.fr/archeoscope/index.htm, 1st weekend in Feb-11 Nov daily 0900-1730 (Jul-Aug till 1830). €9, €4.50 aged 18-25 years, under 18s free*, all about the history and construction of the abbey will appeal to adults and children alike.

Avranches → *For listings, see page 88.*

For more than 1000 years the story of this attractive town on a slope above the River Sée has been linked to that of Le Mont-St-Michel. The far end of its colourful Jardin des Plantes (created over 200 years ago, but re-laid after wartime damage) gives an ethereal view across the expanse of the Sée estuary and the Baie du Mont St-Michel with the enigmatic form of Le Mont-St-Michel rising in the distance. The fortified old town is at the top of the hill, where picturesque narrow streets converge on Place Daniel-Huet. There was once a cathedral behind the square, but it collapsed in 1794. Where it stood is now a garden known as La Plate-Forme, and from here the vista towards the bay is even wider. From this spot Bishop Aubert envisioned an abbey standing on Mont Tombe, which was to become Le Mont-St-Michel.

Avranches is the official repository for the abbey's many precious medieval manuscripts at Le Scriptorial d'Avranches – **Musée des Manuscrits du Mont-St-Michel** ① *place d'Estouteville, T02 33 79 57 00, scriptorial.fr, Tue-Sun Oct-Apr 1000-1230 and 1400-1700, May-Sep till 1800, Jul-Aug no midday closing, closed Jan, last entry an hour before closing, €7, €5* *over-60s, €3 unemployed and students, under-10s free, audioguide additional €3.* This is also a fun and interactive place where visitors can learn about writing and books in general, and the abbey's manuscripts in particular.

There is also an **information office** ⓘ *rue Général de Gaulle, T02 33 58 00 22, ot avranches.com.*

Le Mont-St-Michel listings

For hotel and restaurant price codes and other relevant information, see pages 13-17.

⬤ Where to stay

Le Mont-St-Michel *p84*

€€€€-€€ La Mère Poulard, Grand'Rue, T02 33 89 68 68, merepoulard.com. You are paying for location, not service or facilities, at this adequately comfortable traditional establishment at the entrance to Grand'Rue, associated with the famous restaurant of the same name. It can be a slog up the stairs to your room, rewarded by views of the bay.

€ La Digue, at the mainland end of the causeway, T02 33 60 14 02, ladigue.eu. Ivy clad, inexpensive and almost as close to Le Mont as you can get without actually being there, this heavily used hotel owned by La Mère Poulard provides a well-located base. Most rooms are on the small side with basic facilities. Some look towards Le Mont, as does the restaurant, where fresh local seafood is on the menu.

Avranches *p86*

€€ La Croix d'Or, 83 rue de la Constitution, T02 33 58 04 88, hotel-restaurant-avranches-croix-dor.com. Closed 3 weeks in Jan. A spick-and-span classic family-run small hotel, amiable and helpful, this half-timbered former 17th-century inn gives excellent value for money. Accommodation is simple but attractive and well-maintained. There's a delightful garden, free Wi-Fi and a good restaurant too.

€€-€ Au Jardin des Plantes, place du Jardin des Plantes, T02 33 58 03 68, hotel-restaurant-avranches.com. Well placed for the Jardin des Plantes, some rooms with distant views of Le Mont-St-Michel, this calm, family-run hotel is in 2 sections. It offers a friendly welcome and simple classic rooms, with basic comforts. The hotel's restaurant serving traditional French cuisine is popular with locals.

⬤ Restaurants

Le Mont-St-Michel *p84*

€€€-€€ La Mère Poulard, Grand'Rue, T02 33 89 68 68, merepoulard.com. Daily lunch and dinner. Its name apparently a play on words meaning Mother Hen, this spacious and convivial 2-room traditional restaurant, its walls covered with pictures of notable former clients, is surely the 2nd most famous address in Le Mont-St-Michel after the abbey itself. Long acclaimed by gourmets for its huge, creamy omelettes, it also serves generous *fruits de mer*, lamb, and a wide range of other dishes. Prices, though, are absurdly high for food of this standard.

Avranches *p86*

€€ La Croix d'Or, 83 rue de la Constitution, T02 33 58 04 88, hotel-restaurant-avranches-croix-dor.com. Closed 3 weeks in Jan. Daily lunch and dinner, except Sun dinner from 15 Oct-31 Mar. Bare stone, wooden beams and polished copper pots and pans give rustic charm to this excellent restaurant in a half-timbered 17th-century coaching inn. Tables are laid with white cloths, and the food, emphasizing Normandy specialities, is exceptional. Menus include both cheese and dessert.

€€-€ Au Jardin des Plantes, place du Jardin des Plantes, T02 33 58 03 68, hotel-restaurant-avranches.com. With varied dining areas, including a covered terrace by the pavement, this much-liked restaurant in a hotel near the Jardin des Plantes has an appealing blue and peach colour scheme and a good range of menus. The cuisine is traditional French, with such dishes as *tripes* or *foie gras*.

Contents

Footprint features

Dieppe to Le Havre

Dieppe

Dieppe's old town lies on a narrow spit of land between the lively, crowded, picturesque harbour with its quaysides on one side, and the 2-km-long pebble beach backed by greensward on the other. Agreeable, traffic-free Grand'Rue, reaching from restaurant-lined Quai Henri IV to place du Puits Salé, is the heart of the old town, and here Dieppe's colourful Saturday morning market is held. Originally an 11th-century Viking port – the name comes from the Norse word for 'deep' – Dieppe became one of the busiest sea ports in France. The imposing Château, overlooking the beach on lofty cliffs behind the town, is a remnant of medieval fortifications. In the 16th century Dieppe was home to Jehan Ango's notorious privateer fleet of 100 ships, but even then it had a recreational quality, and was among the first places in Europe to attract 'tourists'. Henry III visited the town in 1578 to bathe in the sea, laying the foundation of its later reputation. Visits for the same purpose by Queen Hortense of Holland, in 1813, and the influential young Duchess of Berry, every year from 1824 to 1830, gave it the seal of approval for European royalty and high society throughout the 19th century. In the early 20th, it took on a more raffish air. Many artists and writers took up residence, and a community of some 3000 wealthy British expats settled here. No longer so glamorous or fashionable, the town remains lively and attractive, and still attracts crowds of Parisian weekenders.

Arriving in Dieppe

Getting there

Bus station ⓘ *Blvd Clémenceau, T02 35 06 69 33.*

Train station ⓘ *Blvd Clémenceau, T02 35 06 69 33.* For details of regional and national rail services, see page 11.

Getting around

The docks, beach, and town centre of Dieppe all make up a small area that can be crossed on foot in about 20 minutes. For journeys further afield, the greater urban area of Dieppe and its five surrounding suburban villages (Arques-la-Bataille, Hautot-sur-Mer, Martin-Eglise, Rouxmesnil-Bouteilles and St-Aubin-sur-Scie) can all be reached on town buses run by **Stradibus**. The two principal stops in the town centre are the railways station and Pont Ango, between which there are buses every few minutes. A single journey costs €1. A carnet of 10 tickets costs €8.60. Information from **Espace Stradibus** ⓘ *56 quai Duquesne, T02 32 14 03 03, infotransports.free.fr/reseaux/dieppe/informations.htm, Mon-Fri 0800-1200 and 1330-1830, Sat 0900-1200.*

Tourist information

There is a **tourist information office** ⓘ *Pont Jehan Ango, T02-32 14 40 60, dieppetourisme. com. Daily May-Sep (Oct-Apr, closed Sun). Mon-Sat hours are Oct-Feb 0900-1230, 1330-1700; Feb-Jun, and Sep 0900-1300, 1400-1800; Jul-Aug 0900-1900. Sun hours are 0930-1300, 1400-1730.*

Places in Dieppe → *For listings, see pages 94-97.*

Château-Musée

ⓘ *Rue de Chastes, T02 35 06 61 99. Jun-Sep 1000-1200 and 1400-1000, Oct-May Wed-Mon 1000-1200 and 1400-1700. €4, €2 concessions, under 12s free.*

Rising on a cliff at Dieppe's western edge, the flint and sandstone Château dominates the town. It has been so damaged, repaired, altered and expanded over the centuries that it's hard to imagine the original fortress built here in the 10th century by Richard the Fearless, Duke of Normandy. The oldest part is the 10th- to 12th-century west tower; the main structure is largely 15th century, though its northwest tower dates from the 14th century and the curtain walls were extended in the 17th century to incorporate the square 13th-century St-Rémy Tower. The structure survived bombardment by the British in 1694 and 1942, and is today the town's museum, divided into sections covering different themes.

The principal exhibition is of 16th- to 19th-century Dieppe ivories. The town was renowned for its skilled ivory carvers, whose clever, intricate work is still a delight to see: statues, model ships, boxes and miniature portraits, as well as a multitude of ornaments, tools and household objects. Several of the finer pieces are copies of well-known sculptures or popular images of their day, such as the lovely 18th-century *Four Seasons*.

Other sections deal with the maritime history of the town, and there are many good paintings, often on a Dieppe waterfront theme, by artists who frequented the town, including Renoir, Sisley, Sickert, Pissarro, Dufy, Courbet and many others, with a separate section devoted to lithographs by Georges Braque.

Oscar Wilde's Dieppe

It was to Dieppe that Oscar Wilde fled on being released from prison in 1897. Many old friends and acquaintances were here, including James McNeill Whistler, Walter Sickert and Aubrey Beardsley, and the art critic Robert Ross, to whom he handed the manuscript of *De Profundis*. He perhaps believed he would be welcomed, but it is said that most of the Dieppe community, including many former friends, shunned him, embarrassed by his imprisonment for homosexuality. His favourite haunts were the big and lively Café des Tribunaux that dominates place du Puits Salé, and quiet Café Suisse on the Arcade la Bourse quayside – both are still there. Wilde moved to Berneval-sur-Mer, 10 km away, then an isolated cliff-top village, to work on *The Ballad of Reading Gaol*.

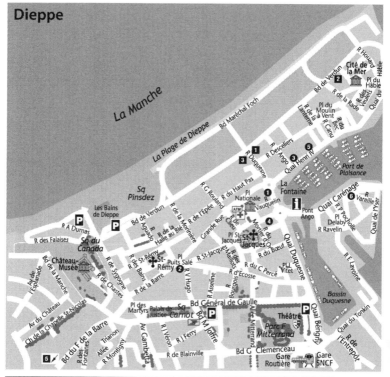

Dieppe

Cité de la Mer

ⓘ *37 rue de l'Asile Thomas, T02 35 06 93 20, estrancitedelamer.fr. Daily 1000-1200 and 1400-1800. €5.80, €4.50 concessions, €3.50 4-16 years.*

Don't imagine a lavish sealife centre – despite the name, this modest rainy day museum is scientific and technical, and mainly devoted to maritime rather than marine life. Most exhibits and displays deal with boat building and fishing, and explain all about tides and sea currents and their impact on the coast.

Right bank

The animated popular quaysides of Dieppe are on the port's west side – the left bank of the River Arques from which the harbour was carved. Cross the two bridges – Pont Ango and Pont Colbert – to the right bank to reach the little district of Le Pollet, a cluster of lanes of old redbrick and flint cottages that make up the fishermen's quarter. Climb up from here to one of the town's most distinctive landmarks, visible from far out at sea – the sailors' small cliff-top chapel, **Notre-Dame de Bon Secours**. This quiet, touching place of prayer, overlooking the harbour, is also a place of remembrance. It contains a memorial to every Dieppe seaman lost at sea since 1876, including whole trawlers missing with all their crew.

200 metres
200 yards

Where to stay 🛏
Hôtel Aguado **1**
Hôtel de l'Europe **2**
Hôtel de la Plage **3**
Villa des Capucins **4**
Villa Florida **5**

Restaurants, bars & clubs 🍷
A La Marmite Dieppoise **4**
Café Suisse **1**
Café des Tribunaux **2**
Chez le Gros **3**
La Musardière **5**
Le Bistrot du Pollet **6**
Les Voiles d'Or **7**

Eglise St-Jacques

ⓘ *22 rue Boucherie, T02 32 14 63 00. Usually open during the day, free.*

Dieppe's large parish church, between Grand'Rue and the fishing port, is a striking Flamboyant presence in the town. It has been much damaged and repaired over the centuries, yet remains an attractive example of the evolution of Gothic architecture from the 13th to 16th centuries, and serves as a monument to Dieppe's past prosperity. There's a good rose window over the central doorway. The interior is worn and damaged, but in use. Frescoes of the Stations of the Cross survive on pillars. The high nave of pale stone dates from the origins of the building, while the elaborate side chapels at the eastern end are the final touches. In one of the side chapels, a memorial honours those who died on the ill-fated Dieppe raid in 1942. Out of keeping with the rest is a remarkable Renaissance carved frieze, thought to have been rescued from Jehan Ango's own private palace when it was destroyed by British bombardment in 1694. The carvings show native people of Brazil and the Caribbean, probably encountered by Ango on his voyages.

Dieppe raid: Operation Jubilee

On 19 August 1942, more than 5000 Canadian commandos and 1000 British launched a surprise attack on Dieppe and the neighbouring coast between Varengeville and Berneval. With considerable air and navy support, their objective was to breach and destroy German coastal defences, take prisoners, capture German planning documents and gather intelligence. Landing at 0500, they were defeated later the same morning without achieving any useful objectives. By the end of the day more than 1000 of the commandos were dead, over 600 wounded and some 2000 taken prisoner. Their air support lost 106 aircraft, while the Luftwaffe lost 48. Following the catastrophe, the one lesson learned was the strength of German defences on the Channel coast.

Dieppe listings

For hotel and restaurant price codes and other relevant information, see pages 13-17.

🛏 Where to stay

Dieppe *p90, map p92*
€€ Hôtel Aguado, bd de Verdun, T02 35 84 27 00, hoteldieppe.com. Ideally situated just a moment's walk from the port, the town centre and the beach, this popular, inexpensive and rather dated 3-star straddles a side street. The main attraction is its position, not the amenities. It offers a choice of modest, homely rooms – perhaps a little too well-worn – either facing the beach or facing the town. Friendly and helpful reception.
€€ Hôtel de l'Europe, bd de Verdun, T02 32 90 19 19, hoteldieppe.com. The 2-star **Europe** has an unmissable wood-clad façade. Inside, decor is light and uncluttered, with a beach-resort feel. The spacious, sea-view rooms are smart and comfortably furnished.
€€-€ Hôtel de le Plage, bd de Verdun, T02 35 84 18 28, plagehotel.fr.st. Modernized, attractive and pleasant, this affordable beachfront hotel makes a good base for Dieppe's town centre. Rooms are simple, brightly decorated, and adequately equipped. There's free Wi-Fi throughout.

Chambres d'hôtes
€€ Villa des Capucins, rue des Capucins, T02 35 82 16 52, villa-des-capucins.fr. This charming and attractive red-brick cottage in the evocative Le Pollet area is a cosy guesthouse, near to the heart of things yet away from the bustle of the town centre. It has a lovely garden.
€€ Villa Florida, Chemin du Golf, T02 35 84 40 37, lavillaflorida.com. Perfect for the golf course, this unusual B&B is a chambre d'hôte de charme. It has very comfortable, richly furnished rooms and the proprietor is a keen fan of yoga.

🍴 Restaurants

Dieppe *p90, map p92*
€€ A La Marmite Dieppoise, rue St-Jean, T02 35 84 24 26. Tue-Sat Sun lunch and dinner, Sun lunch, closed 20 Jun-3 Jul, 21 Nov-9 Dec, 8-16 Feb. Tucked away in a little street between the church and the port, the restaurant gives its name to its very own culinary invention, a rich stew of lobster, mussels and several kinds of fish with crème fraîche sauce. Arguably, it's well worth coming to try that speciality dish. The rest of the menu, though, is unremarkable, and prices are on the high side. The best of the desserts is a warm, home-made apple tart with a tasty cream.

Tables are rather close together, and there's sometimes indifferent and chilly service. Decor, relieved by romantic touches like candles, is faux historic, with bare brick, tile floors and beams.

€€ **Chez le Gros**, quai Henri IV, T02 35 82 28 03. Lunch and dinner. Dieppe harbour is packed with modest fish and shellfish restaurants attracting tourists rather than locals. This waterfront wine bar and bistro looks like a plain and simple café, but it's quite an exception – authentic French cooking that's as much about *foie gras* and *magret de canard* as the ubiquitous *moules-frites*.

€€ **Le Bistrot du Pollet**, rue Tête de Boeuf, T02 35 84 68 57. Tue-Sat lunch and dinner, closed 2 weeks in Apr, 2 weeks in Aug, 10 days in Jan. On the island in the harbour, this convivial little bistro packed with diners is a top spot for eating out in Dieppe. Decor is on a seafaring theme. Cooking is good, with plenty of hearty traditional Normandy fare, *dieppoise* sauces, fresh fish and generous portions.

€€ **Les Voiles d'Or**, Chemin de la Falaise, T02 35 84 16 84, lesvoilesdor.fr. Wed-Sat lunch and dinner, Sun lunch, closed 2 weeks end Nov. High on the right bank, near the Notre Dame de Bon Secours chapel, this modern Michelin-starred restaurant is comfortable and stylish, with polished pale wood and hanging *voiles d'or* – golden sails. There are 2 well-prepared set menus, constantly changing as they reflect what's best in the market that day.

€ **La Musardière**, quai Henri IV, T02 35 82 94 14, restaurant-la.com. Feb-Jun and Sep-Dec Wed-Sun lunch and dinner, daily Jul-Aug. Small, brightly lit, here's the classic cheap and cheerful fish and shellfish restaurant on the quayside, with friendly service and affordable set menus.

Cafés and bars
Café des Tribunaux, du Puits Salé, T02 32 14 44 65. The tall, attractive, gabled tavern has been the haunt of many great names

of art and literature, notably Oscar Wilde. It's a smart, well-kept place, with a restored pre-war look inside, where stained-glass panels encircle an upper gallery. There are wrought-iron tables and chairs on the little square outside. It remains a lively, atmospheric, dominant presence in the town centre, with a view on to Grand'Rue. Excellent morning coffee, freshly squeezed orange juice and croissants. A painting of the Café des Tribunaux by Walter Sickert, showing the café as it was in 1890, hangs in the Tate Britain in London.

Café Suisse, arcades de la Bourse, T02 35 84 10 69. Subject of a painting by Walter Sickert in 1914, this one-time haunt of Oscar Wilde – when he wanted to get away from the smart set – survives as a classic local brasserie, popular with locals. At mealtimes it serves simple traditional fare at modest prices. Outdoor tables are under an arcade.

● **Entertainment**

Dieppe *p90, map p92*
Casinos
Grand Casino Dieppe, 3 bd de Verdun, T02 32 14 48 00, casinodieppe.com. Mon-Thu 2100-0300, Fri 2100-0400, Sat 2000-0400, Sun 1600-0300. Near the sea at the foot of the château, Dieppe casino has slot machines and simple, modern gaming tables. It's far from glamorous, but also has 2 restaurants, a piano bar and show theatre with occasional cabaret or entertainment.

Theatre and cinema
Dieppe Scène Nationale (DSN), quai Bérigny, T02 35 82 04 43, dsn.asso.fr. Tue-Sun 1400-1830. At the end of the harbour, this is the principal venue in Dieppe for arts events, stage shows, world music concerts, drama, modern dance and a full programme of arts performances and family entertainment. There's also a cinema showing a wide variety of new art and popular films as well as cinema classics. If you want to see English-

language films, note that 'VO' means a film is shown in its original language.

✿ Festivals

Dieppe *p90, map p92*
Kite festival, the tourist office for the latest festival information, or visit dieppe-cerf-volant.org. Filling the sky with scores of curious shapes and wild colours, Dieppe Kite Festival is held in **Sep in even-numbered years**, and attracts kite-flying experts from all over the world.

✪ Shopping

Dieppe *p90, map p92*
Food and drink
Epicier Olivier, rue St-Jacques, T02 35 84 22 55, olivierdieppe.com. Tue-Sat 0800-1230 and 1400-1915, Sat no lunchtime closing, Mon afternoons in Jul-Aug. This respected *épicerie fine* with its traditional tiled façade specializes in the best of fine foods. Cheeses are a speciality, but you'll find here too butter sold off the block, fromage blanc and crème fraîche ladled from tubs, as well as coffees, teas, Calvados and local produce. Service is brisk but helpful.

Market
Dieppe's traditional Sat market attracts shoppers from across the region. Stalls run the length of Grand'Rue into place du Puits Salé, place Nationale, place St-Jacques, rue St-Jacques and the side streets. You'll find fresh produce from farms and fishing boats, fine displays of farm-made butter, charcuterie and cheeses (especially the local treat, Neufchâtel), baked goods, farm cider and apple juice, flowers, and stalls selling cooked dishes, especially hot roasted free-range chicken. Many of the fruit and vegetables are bio (organic). Other stalls offer honey and conserves, leather goods, kitchenware, CDs, souvenirs and clothes.

◑ What to do

Dieppe *p90, map p92*
Fishing
Quayside firms run fishing trips and sea cruises. Ask at the tourist office for latest details.

Golf
Golf de Dieppe-Pourville, 51 route de Pourville, T02 35 84 25 05, golf-dieppe.com. Daily all year 0900-1800. This renowned high-quality 18-hole golf course was established as long ago as 1897. Considered a fairly challenging course, it hosts competitions Mar-Oct.

Petit Train tour
Petit Train Touristique de Dieppe, quai Henri-IV (beside tourist office), T02 35 04 56 08. mid May-mid Oct, 1130-1730. €6, €4 child (3-10). All aboard for a fun ride around town. The tour lasts about 1 hr and takes in the beach and town centre sights.

Thermal baths
Les Bains des Docks, Quai de la Réunion, T02 32 79 29 55, vert-marine.com/les-bains-des-docks-le-havre-76. Sep-Jun Mon and Wed 0900-2100, Tue, Thu and Fri 1200-2100, Sat-Sun 0900-1900; Jul-Aug daily 1000-2000. €5.30, €4.30 child 8-12 (under 8s free). Aqua-gym open only for certain periods during the day Mon-Sat. This beautiful gleaming white dockside public baths was designed by a leading modern architect, Jean Nouvel. It has several indoor and outdoor pools of different temperatures, including a heated outdoor Olympic pool, as well as sports and play areas, an 'aqua-gym' for fitness sessions in the water and treatment rooms.

Dieppe *p90, map p92*
Hospital Centre Hospitalier de
Dieppe, av Pasteur, T02 32 14 76 76,
ch-dieppe.fr. **Pharmacy** The most
centrally located pharmacy is La Grande
Pharmacie, 15-17 place Nationale,
T02 35 84 11 20. pharmacie-dieppe.com.

Côte d'Albâtre

Stretching along the whole length of the Seine Maritime seafront, this coast is called the Côte d'Albâtre (Alabaster Coast) simply because alabaster is so white. The chalky plateau of the Pays de Caux reaches the English Channel in an abrupt, majestic line of soaring white cliffs. Sometimes they jut into the sea, sometimes they are set back behind coves and beaches, and sometimes, where there are deep cuts and breaks in the chalk, fishing ports have prospered. The harbours at the foot of the cliffs were established long ago – Fécamp, for example, has been a busy port since Roman times. Several beach resorts also sprang up along the Côte d'Albâtre more than a century ago and have remained popular, such as Etretat, best known for the way the waves have eaten its chalky rock into curious shapes. On the top of the white cliffs, lush vegetation grows and quiet little villages watch out over the sea. Over the centuries, most have made their living from both farming and fishing, although many also have a long tradition of well-to-do outsiders building fine villas and mansions as tranquil hideaways. Among the grandest of all is the lavish home of 16th-century privateer Jehan Ango at Varengeville.

Jehan Ango

A shipbuilder's son and, at first, a shipbuilder himself, Jehan (or Jean) Ango was born in Dieppe in 1480. He became one of the many great seafaring traders and adventurers of the town, making frequent expeditions to Africa and the Americas. This represented a challenge to the Portuguese, who maintained that they alone had the right to trade off the African coast. Ango built a vast fortune, initially through the piracy of captains he equipped and sponsored, notably Jean Fleury, who seized Aztec treasures being taken from Mexico to Spain.

François I, the French king, wishing to respond to the Portuguese dominance in Atlantic trade, authorized Ango to seize all Portuguese trading vessels he encountered in the Atlantic. Jehan Ango's huge fleet of up to 100 vessels proceeded to terrorize Atlantic shipping, seizing 300 Portuguese trading vessels and their cargo. Ships of other nations, including England and Holland, were also seized. Jehan Ango's fortune increased to royal levels, and the king appointed him Governor of Dieppe. He built two homes, one in Dieppe and one (which survives) in Varengeville. His eminent house guests included François I himself, who made Ango a Viscount. However, the king also felt himself entitled to call on Ango's fortune, and pressed him for such large loans that by the end of his life Ango had little left. He died in 1551 and was buried in Dieppe's Eglise St-Jacques.

Varengeville-sur-Mer → For listings, see pages 102-104.

A pretty wooded cliff-top area of hidden cottages, gardens, footpaths and villas, Varengeville is a delight. Arriving from nearby Dieppe, 8 km east, a sign points from the road into a lane between an avenue of trees, leading to the Manoir d'Ango, the grand home of the privateer Jehan Ango, who grew rich by seizing hundreds of Portuguese, English and other merchant vessels (see box, above). Although arranged in the form of a traditional Normandy fortified farm enclosure, the building is in 16th-century Italian Renaissance style, with raised arched galleries forming a loggia on one side, and plenty of fine decoration. In black and white stone, it's arranged around an impressive courtyard at the centre of which is a huge dovecote. Only the grounds may be visited (March to November).

Another lane leads through the trees to the **Parc des Moutiers** ① *T02 35 85 10 02, boisdesmoutiers.com, mid-Mar to mid-Nov, 1000-2000, but ticket office open 1000-1200, 1400-1800, €10, children (7-15) €4)*, 9 ha of cleverly laid out botanic gardens, with rare trees, flowering bushes and sea views. The park is mostly the work of English landscape gardener Gertrude Jekyll (1843-1932). There's always something in bloom, from March to November. Paths wind among colourful flowering bushes and extraordinary 6-m-high rhododendrons. An unusual mansion at the centre of the park, with curious corner windows and many English country house touches, was built in 1898 by the great Imperial architect Sir Edwin Lutyens.

Perhaps the loveliest sight in Varengeville is the lonely little parish church, Eglise de St-Valéry, perched on the edge of a high cliff rising from the seashore. There's a magnificent view of the coast from here. Inside the simple church it's immediately obvious that the building dates from two very different periods, as two naves and two choirs have been stuck together, one 11th-century Romanesque, of pale stone, and one 13th to 15th-century Gothic, partly in brick. Round arches with strangely carved columns separate the two sections. In the south choir aisle is a beautiful modern stained-glass window depicting *The Tree of Jesse*, by the leading Cubist artist Georges Braque, who lived in Varengeville.

The church is surrounded by its simple cemetery, in which Braque (1883-1963) is buried beside his wife. Nearby are several other interesting graves, including that of the composer Albert Roussel (1869-1937).

St-Valéry-en-Caux → *For listings, see pages 102-104.*

After being destroyed during the British retreat to Dunkirk, St-Valéry, 34 km south of Dieppe on D925, was rebuilt and is today a thriving fishing port and marina, overlooked by large modern hotel. The town's new church, built in 1963, has a striking wall of stained glass. There's a **tourist information office** ① *quai d'Amont, T02 35 97 00 63, plateaudecauxmaritime.com.*

The coast and countryside nearby are impressive and beautiful. On the beach, magnificent white cliffs rise up, while climbing from the shore in places are pretty villages and lanes, for example at Veules-les-Roses. At the roadside in Veules a memorial commemorates 38 Commonwealth soldiers who died in 1940 during the unsuccessful Dieppe Raid.

Fécamp → *For listings, see pages 102-104.*

Although a busy, industrial fishing port, Fécamp, 30 km north of Le Havre on D940, is also an old resort town, enclosed by white cliffs. It provides the background to several novels by Guy de Maupassant, who was born here. The harbour is the town's focal point, and here a good deal of France's daily catch of fresh cod is landed. The town rises steeply from the waterfront. There's a good market in the town centre on Saturdays, centred on place Bellet. There is a **tourist information office** ① *Quai Sadi Carnot, T02 35 28 51 01, fecamptourisme.com.*

Eglise Abbatiale de la Trinité
① *Place des Ducs Richard, T02 35 28 84 39. Approx Apr-Sep 0900-1900, Oct-Mar 0900-1200 and 1400-1700.*
Fécamp was put on the map in the early seventh century when pilgrims flocked to see a lead casket, supposedly containing 'drops of the Holy Blood', which had been washed ashore in the hollowed-out trunk of what was said to be a fig tree. A monastery was built to protect the Precious Blood, as it became known. In the 11th century, Richard II of England built the Eglise de la Trinité to house the relic. He also re-founded the monastery as a huge abbey, the first under Benedictine rule. It grew immensely wealthy as vast numbers of pilgrims came to revere the Precious Blood.

The abbey church was later reconstructed in Flamboyant Gothic style, and has been much altered over the centuries, but still contains some lovely vestiges of the original. It is a huge building, its white stone interior tall and soaring in design and, at 127 m, one of the longest churches in Europe. Here you'll find the tombs of both Duke Richard I and Duke Richard II, as well as some superb stone carving and notable artworks, especially the richly detailed 15th-century *Dormition of the Virgin*. Along the length are many side chapels. Even today, pilgrims come here to see the Precious Blood, in the small, carved white marble *Tabernacle du Précieux Sang*.

Palais Bénédictine

① 110 rue Alexandre le Grand, T02 35 10 26 10, benedictine.fr. Daily 1030-1245 and 1400-1800, slightly longer hours in summer, shorter in winter (closed 1 Jan-10 Feb), €7.20, €3.20 child, under 12s free.

In the 16th century, Fécamp's Benedictine community used local wild plants to create their very own liqueur, and called it, quite simply, Bénédictine. The abbey's distillery soon became, and still is, a thriving business, since 1863 unconnected to the monks. Today the distilling takes place in a wildly ornate 19th-century mock-Gothic palace called the Palais Bénédictine, which also houses an eclectic museum on the history of the Benedictines and their liqueur. In the museum, astonishing displays include precious ivories, a 15th-century illuminated Book of Hours, and several painted panels of the same period, finely worked silver and gold, priceless alabaster pieces, ancient manuscripts, a collection of paintings dating back to the 14th century, and a gallery of modern art. Afterwards, pop into the airy tasting room to the right of the entrance for a tot of rich, sweet, acerbic Bénédictine (free with your entry ticket, or €2 without).

Etretat → For listings, see pages 102-104

The great feature of this long-established small resort, 29 km north of Le Havre on D940, which is popular with weekenders all year round, is its green-topped white cliffs, carved into curious shapes by long millennia of wind and waves. Most striking, cut out of the chalk of the Falaise d'Aval at the south end of the beach, is a tall offshore needle of white rock called the Aiguille; and the Porte d'Aval, a natural archway that looks like an elephant's trunk sticking into the water. At the north end, the charming little 11th- and 12th-century Notre-Dame de la Garde chapel stands alone on top of the spectacular Falaise d'Amont cliff, which looks like a small open doorway in a huge white wall in the sea. Clearly marked (but steep) cliff footpaths allow you to fully appreciate the beauty and grandeur of the setting. A pleasant promenade behind the beach runs part of the way between the two cliffs. South of town, the Manneport, another curious archway in the sea, can be reached on a cliff-top path, which is a section of long-distance footpath GR21.

In the late 19th and early 20th century, Etretat was one of those thoroughly elegant little Normandy seaside resorts patronized by the most distinguished people. Its breezy marine freshness adding to its appeal. While those days are long gone, the town remains bright and busy, and preserves a refined air. There's a golf course and a casino. In town, place du Marché is wonderfully picturesque, with a wooden former covered market. There is a tourist information office on place Maurice Guillard, T02 35 27 05 21, etretat.net.

Well-known artists and writers also came frequently to Etretat in its heyday. Guy de Maupassant, who spent his teenage years here, later took his family for summer holidays at Etretat. Victor Hugo and Gustave Flaubert both declared how much they loved the Etretat seaside, and stream of Impressionists came here to paint, among them Monet, Courbet, Delacroix and Degas.

Côte d'Albâtre listings

For hotel and restaurant price codes and other relevant information, see pages 13-17.

🛏 Where to stay

Varengeville-sur-Mer *p99*

€ La Terrasse, de Vasterival, T02 35 85 12 54, hotel-restaurant-la-terrasse.com. Quiet, comfortable, friendly accommodation tucked away in countryside on the cliff top at the western edge of Varengeville, this country-house style hotel has fine views of the sea. Decor is simple and modern. There's a very attractive restaurant with good cooking, see below.

Fécamp *p100*

€€€ Grand Pavois, quai Vicomte, T02 35 10 01 01, hotel-grand-pavois.com. A smart 3-star hotel overlooking the harbour, the Grand Pavois has generously sized rooms with plain and simple modern furnishings and decor. Some have a particularly fine view. There's a relaxing piano bar on the ground floor.

€€ Hôtel Normandy, 4 av Gambetta, T02 35 29 55 11, normandy-fecamp.com. Simple and unpretentious modern comfort is on offer for very modest prices in this white-fronted former coaching inn standing beside the church of St-Etienne, on a corner near the port. Some rooms have sea views. Downstairs is the restaurant and brasserie Le Maupassant, see page 103.

€€-€ Mer, bd Albert 1er, T02 35 28 24 64, hotel-dela-mer.com. This unpretentious modern 2-star is right on the beachfront, with the children's play area next door, and right above a busy brasserie. The casino is not far away. Rooms are simply but pleasantly decorated and adequately equipped, some with sea views and balcony, though the rear rooms have a less pleasant prospect. There's free Wi-Fi.

Etretat *p101*

€€€ Domaine St-Clair – Le Donjon, Chemin de St-Clair, T02 35 27 08 23, ledonjon-etretat.fr. Luckily donjon means not 'dungeon', but 'keep', rather a grandiose name for this splendid Anglo-Norman country house and belle epoque holiday villa with views across the town to the sea. Rooms are comfortably equipped and very varied; most are large – vast would be a better description in some cases. The hotel stands in its own attractive grounds, and has a heated pool, a library and an elegant gourmet restaurant. There is golf and riding nearby.

€€€-€€ Dormy House, du Havre, T02 35 27 07 88, etretat-hotel.com. A cliff-edge position with wonderful views adds to the appeal of this handsome 19th-century manor house in its own grounds. Rooms are spacious and comfortable, varying from relatively simple to luxurious, so there's a big price range. Standard rooms look out on the grounds, while superior rooms have a sea view. The hotel has an excellent restaurant, see page 103.

€€-€ Manoir de la Salamandre/ La Résidence, bd Coty, T02 35 27 02 87, hotelresidenceetretat.com.This picturesque half-timbered manor house preserves numerous historic touches, exposed beams, polished wood and 4-poster beds. Rooms are charming and adequately equipped, very varied in size, some presented as family rooms. The ground floor is Restaurant la Salamandre.

🍴 Restaurants

Varengeville-sur-Mer *p99*

€€ La Terrasse, de Vasterival, T02 35 85 12 54, hotel-restaurant-la-terrasse.com. Daily lunch and dinner. In the Hôtel la Terrasse (see above) this attractive, spacious restaurant, hung with pale fabrics, has lovely views out to sea. The accomplished and skilful menus focus on fresh local fish and shellfish, with dishes like mussels in roquefort sauce, local specialities such as *sole à la dieppoise*, and favourite desserts such as tarte tatin.

Fécamp *p100*

€€ Auberge de la Rouge, route du Havre (corner of rue Bois de Boclon), 2 km from Fécamp, T02 35 28 07 59, auberge-rouge.fr. Tue-Sat 1215-1330 and 1915-2100, Sun 1915-2100. In the pretty, rustic setting of a flower-decked old coaching inn there are plenty of wooden beams and exposed brick. Here good traditional French cooking is served in 3 cosy dining rooms, using all the best ingredients of the market.

€€-€ Le Maupassant, av Gambetta, T02 35 29 55 11, normandy-fecamp.com. Mon-Sat all day. On the ground floor of the Hôtel Normandy (see page 102), this popular restaurant and brasserie serves classic French and Normandy fare, such as foie gras followed by cod in cream sauce, with some well-priced set menus.

€€-€ Le Vicomte, rue Président R Coty, T02 35 28 47 63. Mon-Tue, Thu-Sat for lunch and dinner, closed end Apr and beginning May, 2 weeks in Aug, Christmas and New Year. Tasty, classic French bistro cooking is served at this busy, appealing little place not far from the port area. What you'll be offered all depends on what's best in the market – menus of the day are written on a blackboard.

Etretat *p101*

€€ Dormy House, du Havre, T02 35 27 07 88, etretat-hotel.com. Lunch and dinner. The restaurant in this cliff-edge hotel on the south side of town has magnificent sea views, and a choice of tempting set menus. Dishes are delicate and imaginative, with plenty of fresh fish and local touches, such as fresh cod open ravioli with mushrooms and leeks cooked with cider and shellfish sauce. Desserts include roast apricots with lavender ice cream.

€€ Le Bicorne, 5 bd Président R Coty, T02 35 29 62 22, hws.fr/lebicorne. Thu-Mon for lunch and dinner (daily in school holidays). In a warm and cosy setting of polished timber and wood panels, excellent fish and seafood dishes – and plenty of classic meat dishes as well – are presented in striking, colourful arrangements. Try the monkfish with pommeau sauce. Service is warm and genuine.

€€-€ La Salamandre, bd Coty, T02 35 27 17 07, lasalamandreetretat.com. Lunch and dinner. In a picturesque half-timbered manor house in the town centre, the restaurant of this small hotel has rustic, cosy decor of exposed beams, polished wood and gingham cloths. Everything served is certified organic, or is the fresh catch of the day. Dishes have a simple, natural quality, such as 3 fresh fish grilled with olive oil, and there's a vegetarian selection.

⊕ Entertainment

Etretat *p101*
Casinos
JOA Casino, 1 rue Adolphe Boissaye, T02 35 27 00 54, joa-casino.com/casinos-loisirs/casino-joa-d-etretat. Daily 1000-0100 (0300 Fri, Sat and eve of national holidays). With a pub-like feel, Etretat's casino has slot machines, some simple gaming tables, a bar and restaurant, as well as a programme of evening entertainment like a disco or jazz. The best feature is its position on the beach, with views towards the arch cliffs.

⊙ Shopping

Palais Bénédictine *p101*
Food and drink
110 rue Alexandre le Grand, T02 35 10 26 10, benedictine.fr. Early Feb to Mar and mid-Oct to 31 Dec 1030-1145, 1400-1700; Apr to early Jul and end Aug to mid-Oct 1000-1200, 1400-1730; early Jul to end Aug 1000-1800. Closed Jan-early Feb. The Benedictine distillery has its own boutique

selling bottles of the liqueur, and a selection of unusual treats and delicacies filled or flavoured with it, such as 12 chocolates filled with Benedictine.

⚠ What to do

Fécamp *p100*
Boat tours
Ask at the tourist office for their choice of 2-hr mini-cruises giving views of the coast and port.

Etretat *p101*
Golf
Golf d'Etretat, route du Havre, T02 35 27 04 89, golfetretat.com. Apr-Aug 0830-1900 daily (except as affected by special events and competitions), Sep-Oct Wed-Mon 0900-1800, Nov-Mar Wed-Mon 0900-1700. On top of high chalk cliffs beside Etretat, with their dramatic arches stepping into the waves, is spread the green expanse of the town's golf course. Founded in 1908, it soon became prestigious: many of its members were British aristocrats. It is still highly rated, in a remarkable setting, and the clubhouse has an excellent restaurant.

❶ Directory

Fécamp *p100*
Hospital Centre Hospitalier Intercommunal du Pays des Hautes Falaises, 100 ave du Président Mitterrand, T02 35 10 90 00, ch-fecamp.fr.
Pharmacy Pharmacie de la Marine, 65 Quai Bérigny, T02 35 28 00 68.

Le Havre

Le Havre 100 years ago was a bustling, picturesque sea port and the home of the first Impressionists – some of their views of it can be seen in the important Musée Malraux. Today, thanks to its vast industrial areas, travellers often take the view that Le Havre is a place to get away from rather than go to. Nor is it Le Havre's fault that the 16th-century town was almost completely destroyed by Allied bombing in September 1944 (killing more than 4000 residents in one week) and had to be quickly and cheaply rebuilt. However, the rebuilding was entrusted to Auguste Perret, a 70-year-old follower of the architect Le Corbusier who shared his passion for reinforced concrete. Perret's vision resulted in a Quartier Moderne at the heart of the city laid out as an evenly spaced grid of long straight streets lined with not unattractive but monotonously similar buildings, often the same height along any given street – nearly all five, six or seven storeys high, with a profusion of balconies. There is occasional relief in the form of broad avenues, squares and parks. Le Havre also has a pleasant sand and pebble beach backed by gardens, and a charming, bustling waterfront, close to the main street, avenue Foch. Whether Auguste Perret's Le Havre is a success remains controversial. Nevertheless, in 2005 it was named a World Heritage Site.

Arriving in La Havre

Getting there
The **Gare Routière** is at Boulevard de Strasbourg, T02 35 26 67 23, and the train station at **Cours Lafayette/Cours République**, T02 35 22 35 00.

Getting around
Within the greater urban area of Le Havre, an extensive public transport network of buses (including six all-night routes) and two modern tramlines is operated from early in the morning until late in the evening by **LiA (Les Lignes de l'Agglo)** ① *T02-35 22 35 00, transports-lia.fr.*

Tourist information
There's a **tourist information office** ① *186 blvd Clémeneceau, T02 32 74 04 04, lehavretourisme.com, Mon-Sat 0900-1900, Sun 1000-1230 and 1430-1800, Nov-Easter closes 1830 weekdays, mornings only on Sun.*

Places in Le Havre → *For listings, see pages 108-110.*

Musée des Beaux Arts – André Malraux
① *2 bd Clemenceau, T02 35 19 62 62. muma-lehavre.fr/blog-50ans. Wed-Mon 1100-1800 (1900 Sat-Sun), closed national holidays. €5, €3 concessions, under 26s free.*
Built overlooking the waterside at the very mouth of the Seine, the glass and steel museum – with a large concrete sculpture in front – offers a cool, light-filled space to display a superb collection of Impressionist and Post-Impressionist artworks from some of its greatest names. Other areas are devoted to painting and sculpture from the 16th-20th centuries and contemporary art. The different galleries are linked by walkways like those on a ship. In particular there are over 200 works by Eugène Boudin, as well as several good examples of Monet, Renoir and Pissarro, and other Impressionists. Among Post-Impressionists, another Le Havre native, the Fauvist Raoul Dufy, is very well represented, with numerous paintings and drawings, many inspired by local life. Other Fauvists on display include Van Dongen and Friesz.

Eglise St-Joseph
① *Bd François 1er, T02 32 74 04 05. Daily 1000-1800 (except during special ceremonies).*
The city's most visible landmark, its distinctive octagonal spire rising to 110 m, has been acclaimed one of Europe's greatest monuments to the post-war reconstruction. This large church, built of concrete and completed in 1957 after Perret's death, is arguably his masterpiece, although whether it can be called beautiful remains debatable. Outwardly the shape resembles a rocket, while the spacious interior seems more like an auditorium than a church. Perret dedicated it to the memory of the victims of the 1944 bombings. He pictured the tall slender spire as a lighthouse – 6500 shards of coloured glass set into the concrete supposedly allowing ever-changing light through the building. This works well on a bright sunny day, which causes a mosaic of colour to be scattered around the angular interior.

Appartement Témoin (the Show Flat)

① 186 bd Clemenceau, T02 35 22 31 22. Tours €3, on Wed, Sat and Sun 1400-1700 (tour starts every hr from 1 place de l'Hôtel de Ville) – book at tourist office.

A rare and fascinating exhibit, Perret's Show Flat reveals the humane ambition that lay behind the architect's designs for the new Le Havre. Many of the revolutionary ideas he incorporated into his apartment blocks have now become normal: plenty of light, built-in kitchens, central heating, and chutes in which to throw rubbish. The flat is furnished with the inexpensive but stylish mass-produced furniture of the early 1950s, and all the latest mod cons of the period.

Ste-Adresse

Spread across the sea cliffs north of the city centre, this lofty, airy residential suburb has good views over the port and out to sea. Here the 19th-century Fort de Ste-Adresse – one of several forts built to defend the Seine estuary – has been laid out as an attractive park and botanic gardens called Les Jardins Suspendus (Hanging Gardens). Ideal for a rest or stroll, it features a wide variety of rare and exotic plants from around the world.

Le Havre listings

For hotel and restaurant price codes and other relevant information, see pages 13-17.

🛏 Where to stay

Le Havre *p105*

€€€ Vent d'Ouest, rue de Caligny, T02 35 42 50 69, ventdouest.fr. In a typical Quartier Moderne building well placed near the main shopping area in avenue Foch and close to the waterfront, this quiet, friendly hotel has a bright marine feel. Rooms are sometimes on the small side, but are comfortably furnished in pine, in an attractive, homely style, especially those equipped with kitchenettes and intended for long stays. The hotel has a useful restaurant and bar.

€€€-€€ Pasino, Jules Ferry, T02 35 26 00 00, casinolehavre.com. Arty, chic and stylish, this comfortable, well-equipped modern hotel is part of the **Casino Partouche**, and has an atmosphere of self-indulgence and pleasure. Rooms are spacious, staff helpful, and there's free Wi-Fi. In addition to its casino, the hotel has 3 restaurants and a luxurious spa (closed Tue and Wed), where you can go straight from your room in a bathrobe.

€€ Art Hôtel (Best Western), rue Louis Brindeau, T02 35 22 69 44, art-hotel.fr. Quirky touches – for example, the elevator made to look like a shower cubicle – enliven the simple, decor at this Quartier Moderne building nearly opposite the entertainment complex Le Volcan. Furnishings are modern, some rooms small, and staff helpful.

€€ Novotel Le Havre Bassin Vauban, cours Lafayette, T02 35 19 23 23, novotel. com. With its blue neon sign illuminating the port near the station, the **Novotel** offers the modern comforts typical of this mid-range, well-priced chain. Interiors are designed to reflect Le Havre's 1950s modernity, and the restaurant aims for a modern style of cuisine.

€€ Terminus, cours de la République, T02 35 25 42 48, grand-hotel-terminus.fr. Ideal for a short stopover, this hotel opposite the railway station is functional and straightforward. It's popular with business travellers, with its reasonable prices, calm atmosphere and soothing, low-key decor. It has its own simple inexpensive restaurant and bar.

€ Richelieu, rue de Paris, T02 35 42 38 71, hotel-lerichelieu-76.com. Looking a little out of place in an arcaded row of shops, this little hotel offers small, basic but homely and comfortable rooms, brightly and individually decorated with tiny bathrooms attached. It has a friendly, genuine feel, is clean and well kept, provides free Wi-Fi and is located in the Quartier Moderne city centre.

🍴 Restaurants

Le Havre *p105*

€€€-€€ Jean-Luc Tartarin, av Foch, T02 35 45 46 20, jeanluc-tartarin.com. Tue-Sat for lunch and dinner. Ambitious gastronomic cuisine has won this acclaimed restaurant a Michelin star. Shellfish is strongly featured. Speciality lobster and young pigeon dishes have striking exotic flavour combinations such as tea, coffee or cocoa. The slick, contemporary decor is in muted pale and dark chocolate tones.

€€ Brasserie Pasino, Jules Ferry, T02 35 26 00 00, casinolehavre.com. Daily 1200-2400. This brasserie with harbour views is 1 of 3 eating places in the **Casino Hotel Partouche**. Affordable menus range from brasserie classics and mixed grills to Normandy specialities.

€€ La Petite Auberge, rue de Ste-Adresse, T02 35 46 27 32, lapetiteauberge-lehavre. fr. Tue-Sun 0900-2300, except Sun dinner and Wed lunch. Closed 3 weeks in summer, 1 week in autumn, 2 weeks in Feb. Towards the heights of Ste-Adresse, this cosy dining room of an old inn has a façade of painted wooden beams, plush decor and furnishing with rich cream and maroon colours and white napery. Fresh market produce is used to make a range of dishes such as rissoles of parma ham and ricotta.

€ **L'Acrobate**, 77 rue Louis Brindeau, T02 35 41 24 42. Mon-Sat 0900-2300. This simple and unassuming city centre brasserie attracts locals for a drink or a bite to eat, and serves good simple French classic dishes on a very reasonably priced set menu.

Cafés and bars

Beer and Billiards, rue René Coty, T02 35 42 44 88. Outside the Quartier Moderne, this pub-like snooker bar is on 2 floors, with a good selection of drinks, 17 billiard tables, and major football matches shown on big TV screens.

Le Chillou, rue Chillou, T02 35 41 75 49. This small, long-established city centre bar can become lively with locals popping in for a drink or a snack. One of its attractions is the patron's warm personality. Another is the daily menu of home-cooked favourites at modest prices.

❶ Bars and clubs

Le Havre *p105*
A fast-changing dance club scene provides late-night entertainment all week. Most clubs are in the docks area, by the Bassin du Commerce.

Wab Bar and Lobby Lounge, 33 rue d'Iéna, T02 35 53 03 91, wablobbylounge.com. Bar open Mon-Sat 1800-0200; Lounge open Thu-Sat 2200-0500. This rather glamorous clubby cocktail bar near the docks is the place to relax with a drink or a meal and enjoy a lounge ambience with an eclectic mix of music from jazz to rock.

❷ Entertainment

Le Havre *p105*
Music
Le Volcan – Le Havre National Stage, Oscar Niemeyer, rue de Paris, T02 35 19 10 10, levolcan.com. Brilliant arts complex inside 2 volcano-shaped structures, the work of architect Oscar Niemeyer (1907–2012; like Auguste Perret, he was fascinated by the possibilities of concrete). They stage performances of modern dance and classical music. From 2011 to 2013, performances were moved to the former Le Havre ferry terminal (known for the duration as Le Volcan Maritime) to allow an extensive renovation of the Volcan buildings. Le Volcan Maritime is at ave. Lucien Corbeaux, T02 35 19 10 20.

❸ Shopping

Le Havre *p105*
St-Vincent area between St-Roch public park and the beach is packed with classy little shops selling haute couture, gourmet specialities, jewellery, art and antiques.

Market
The big, bustling street market in avenue Réné Coty is held every Mon, Wed and Fri.

Shopping centres
Centre Commercial Grand Cap, du Bois au Coq, T02 35 54 71 71, grandcap.fr. Mon-Sat 0930-1930, except Auchan, Mon-Sat 0830-2130. For shopping under one roof, head to the Grand Cap mall on the northern edge of the city. There's an Auchan hypermarket, and much else besides.

Espace Coty, René Coty, T02 32 74 86 87, espacecoty-lehavre.com. Mon-Sat most shops open 0930-2000. The area around ave Foch, rue de Paris and ave René Coty is full of chic fashion, accessories and jewellery stores, as well as top-quality gourmet food specialists, including a branch of **Chocolatier Auzou**. Coty shopping mall has 80 shops on

3 floors, as well as restaurants and cafés, plus a post office and a supermarket.

☺ What to do

Le Havre p105
Cultural tours
Le Havre Ville d'art et d'histoire, 186 bd Clemenceau, T02 35 21 27 33, ville-lehavre.fr. Prices may vary slightly depending on the tour. Approx €5, €3 students, €3 child 12-18, under 12s €3 during summer school holidays, under 12s free at all other times, unemployed free. Visit to the **Appartement Témoin** €3, under 26s free. Le Havre city council and tourist office run a full programme of guided visits to Le Havre's cultural and architectural attractions. Each tour lasts 1-1½ hrs and focuses on a single site or aspect of the city. There are also tours to the **Hanging Gardens** and **Le Volcan arts centre**. The tourist office can provide information and make bookings.

Petit Train tour
Office de Tourisme, 186 bd Clemenceau, T02 32 74 04 04, le-havre-tourism.com. Runs during school holidays only, usually needs to be booked in advance, €5.50, under 13s free. The 'little train' snakes through the city to the sights on a choice of itineraries: for example, **Le Havre World Heritage Site** (1 hr), or **Le Havre Ste-Adresse** (45 mins).

❶ Directory

Le Havre p105
Hospital (for general emergencies) Hôpital J Monod, 29 ave Pierre Mendés-France, Montvilliers, T02 32 73 32 32, ch-havre.fr. **Pharmacy** There are several pharmacies in the town centre, including in the main square, at 26 place de l'Hôtel de Ville (T02 35 42 46 78, pharmacie-havre.fr).

Contents

Footnotes

Language

Basics

hello	*bonjour*
good evening	*bonsoir*
goodbye	*au revoir/salut*
	(polite/informal)
please	*s'il vous plaît*
thank you	*merci*
I'm sorry, excuse me	*pardon, excusez-moi*
yes	*oui*
no	*non*
how are you?	*comment allez-vous?/*
	ça va?
	(polite/informal)
fine, thank you	*bien, merci*
one moment	*un instant*
how?	*comment?*
how much?	*c'est combien?*
when?	*quand?*
where is …?	*où est…?*
why?	*pourquoi?*
what?	*quoi?*
what's that?	*qu'est-ce que c'est?*
I don't understand	*je ne comprends pas*
I don't know	*je ne sais pas*
I don't speak French	*je ne parle pas français*
how do you say …	*comment on dit …*
(in French)?	*(en français)?*
do you speak English?	*est-ce que vous*
	parlez anglais?/
	Parlez-vous anglais?
help!	*au secours!*
wait!	*attendez!*
stop!	*arrêtez!*

Numbers

one	*un*
two	*deux*
three	*trois*
four	*quatre*
five	*cinq*
six	*six*
seven	*sept*
eight	*huit*
nine	*neuf*
10	*dix*
11	*onze*
12	*douze*
13	*treize*
14	*quatorze*
15	*quinze*
16	*seize*
17	*dix-sept*
18	*dix-huit*
19	*dix-neuf*
20	*vingt*
21	*vingt-et-un*
22	*vingt-deux*
30	*trente*
40	*quarante*
50	*cinquante*
60	*soixante*
70	*soixante-dix*
80	*quatre-vingts*
90	*quatre-vingt-dix*
100	*cent*
200	*deux cents*
1000	*mille*

Shopping

this one/that one	*celui-ci/celui-là*
less	*moins*
more	*plus*
expensive	*cher*
cheap	*pas cher/bon marché*
how much is it?	*c'est combien?/ combien ça coûte?*
can I have …? (literally 'I would like) …'	*je voudrais…*

Travelling

one ticket for…	*un billet pour…*
single	*un aller-simple*
return	*un aller retour*
airport	*l'aéroport*
bus stop	*l'arrêt de bus*
train	*le train*
car	*la voiture*
taxi	*le taxi*
is it far?	*c'est loin?*

Hotels

a single/double room	*une chambre à une personne/ deux personnes*
a double bed	*un lit double/ un grand lit*
bathroom	*la salle de bain*
shower	*la douche*
is there a (good) view?	*est-ce qu'il y a une (belle) vue?*
can I see the room?	*est-ce que je peux voir la chambre?*
when is breakfast?	*le petit dejeuner est à quelle heure?*
can I have the key?	*est-ce que je peux avoir la clef?/ La clef, s'il vous plaît*

Time

morning	*le matin*
afternoon	*l'après-midi*
evening	*le soir*
night	*la nuit*
a day	*un jour*
a week	*une semaine*
a month	*un mois*
soon	*bientôt*
later	*plus tard*
what time is it?	*quelle heure est-il?*
today	*aujourd'hui*
tomorrow	*demain*
yesterday	*hier*

Days

Monday	*lundi*
Tuesday	*mardi*
Wednesday	*mercredi*
Thursday	*jeudi*
Friday	*vendredi*
Saturday	*samedi*
Sunday	*dimanche*

Months

January	*Janvier*
February	*février*
March	*mars*
April	*avril*
May	*mai*
June	*juin*
July	*Juillet*
August	*août*
September	*septembre*
October	*octobre*
November	*novembre*
December	*décembre*

Menu reader

General

petit déjeuner	breakfast
déjeuner	lunch
dîner	dinner or supper
hors d'œuvre	appetisers
entrées	starters
plat principal	main course
menu/formule	set menu
plat du jour	dish of the day
carte des vins	wine list

Drinks (*boissons*)

bière	German or Belgian-style beer
cidre bouchée	sparkling cider
cidre doux, cidre sec	dry cider, sweet cider
pommeau	strong apple aperitif
Calvados	apple brandy
apéritif	drink taken before dinner
digestif	*after-dinner drink, usually a liqueur or spirit*
eau gazeuse/pétillante	sparkling/slightly sparkling mineral water
eau plat/minérale	still/mineral water
bouteille	bottle
dégustation	tasting
vin rouge/blanc/rosé	red/white/rosé wine
pichet	jug, used to serve water, wine or cider
une pression	a glass of draught beer
une bière	a beer
un demi	small beer (33cl)
un cidre	cider
un panaché	beer/lemonade shandy
jus de fruit	fruit juice
orange pressée	freshly squeezed orange juice
sirop	fruit syrup or cordial served with water or soda

un coca	Coca-Cola
glaçons	ice cubes
un café	coffee (black espresso)
un (grand) crème	a (large) white coffee
une noisette	espresso with a dash of milk
deca	decaf
chocolat chaud	hot chocolate
lait	milk
un thé	tea, usually served black with a slice of lemon (au citron) – if you want milk ask for un peu de lait froid, a little cold milk
une tisane/infusion	herbal tea

Fruit (*fruits*) and vegetables (*légumes*)

ail	garlic
ananas	pineapple
artichaut	artichoke
asperge	asparagus
blettes	Swiss chard
cassis	blackcurrants
cèpes	porcini mushrooms
champignons de Paris	button mushrooms
châtaignes	chestnuts
chou	cabbage
citron	lemon
citrouille or potiron	pumpkin
cocos	small, white beans
courge	marrow or squash
épinards	spinach
fenouil	fennel
fèves	broad beans
figues	figs
fraises	strawberries
framboises	raspberries
haricots verts	green beans
lentilles vertes	green lentils
mesclun	a mixture of young salad leaves
poires	pears

pomme de terre	potato, primeurs are new potatoes, and frites are chips (chips being crisps)	coquillage	shellfish
		coquilles St Jacques	scallops
		colin	hake
		crevettes	prawns
pommes	apples, the Reinette d'Orléans and Reine des Reinettes are local varieties	dorade	sea bream
		ecrevisses	crayfish
		homard	lobster
		huîtres	oysters
prunes	plums	langoustines	Dublin Bay prawns
truffe	truffle	lotte	monkfish
		loup de mer	sea bass

Sauces and cooking styles

dieppois	with mussels, white wine and cream	maquereau	mackerel
		morue	salt-cod
jus	meat juice with nothing added (may be thickened by reduction)	moules	mussels
		palourdes	a kind of clam
		poissons de rivière	river fish
		poulpe	octopus
matelote Normande	creamy white sauce with cider and calvados	poutine	very tiny, young sardines, most often cooked in an omelette or served raw
Normand(e)	cooked with cider or calvados, and cream added		
		praires	clams
à la Normande	casseroled with apples, calvados and cream	raie	skate
		rascasse	scorpion fish
		rouget	red mullet
		St-Pierre	John Dory
sauce	any kind of sauce or dressing	sardines	sardines
		saumon	salmon
vallée d'Auge	meat flambéed in calvados and served in cream and cider sauce	soupe de poisson	a smooth rockfish-based soup
		soupions	small squid
		thon	tuna
		truite	trout
		turbotin	small turbot

Fish and seafood
(poissons et fruits de mer)

aiglefin	haddock		

Meat (viande) and poultry (volaille)

anchoïade	anchovy-based spread	agneau (pré-salé)	lamb (from saltwater flood meadows)
anchois	anchovies		
anguille	eel	andouillette	soft sausage made from pig's small intestines, usually grilled
bar	bass		
barbue	brill		
bigorneaux	winkles		
bulots	sea snails, whelks	à point	medium cooked meat (or tuna steak), usually still pink inside
cabillaud	cod		
calamar	squid		
coques	cockles	bien cuit	well-cooked

blanquette de veau	veal stew in white sauce with cream, vegetables and mushrooms	pintade	guinea fowl
		porc	pork
		pot-au-feu	slow-cooked beef and vegetable stew
bleu	barely-cooked meat, almost raw	poulet	chicken
bœuf	beef	rillettes	coarse pork pâté
boucherie	butcher's shop or display	rillons	big chunks of pork cooked in pork fat
boudin	black pudding, blood sausage	ris de veau	sweetbreads
		sanglier	wild boar
canard	duck	saucisse	small sausage
charcuterie	encompasses sausages, hams and cured or salted meats	saucisson	salami, eaten cold
		saucisson sec	air-dried salami
		taureau	bull
chevreuil	venison, roe deer	veau	veal
confit	process to preserve meat, usually duck, goose or pork (eg confit de canard)		

Desserts (*desserts*)

		chantilly	whipped, sweetened cream
		compôte	stewed fruit, often as a purée
cuisse de grenouille	frog's leg		
dinde	turkey	crème anglaise	egg custard
escalope	thin, boneless slice of meat	crème brûlée	chilled custard cream dessert
faux-filet	beef sirloin	crème caramel	baked custard flavoured with caramel
foie-gras	fattened goose or duck liver		
fumé(e)	smoked	glace	ice cream
géline de Touraine or la Dame-Noire	grain-fed chicken prized by restaurateurs, awarded a Label Rouge	boules de glace	scoops of ice cream
		le parfum	flavour, when referring to ice cream or yoghurt
		pâtisserie	pastries, cakes and tarts – also the place where they are sold
gigot d'agneau	leg of lamb		
jambon	ham; look for jambon d'Amboise, an especially fine ham	sabayon	creamy dessert made with eggs, sugar and wine or cider
lapin	rabbit	tarte au citron	lemon tart
lardons	small pieces of ham	tarte Normande	apple tart
médaillon	small, round cut of meat or fish	tarte Tatin	upside-down apple tart
mouton	mutton	teurgoule	baked rice pudding sprinkled with cinnamon
pavé	thickly cut steak		

Other

assiette	plate (eg assiette de charcuterie)	*garniture*	garnish, side dish
		gâteau	cake
beurre	butter	*gaufre*	waffle, usually served with chocolate sauce
beurre blanc	buttery white wine sauce often served with fish		
		Hollandaise	rich oil and egg yolk sauce flavoured with lemon juice
boulangerie	bakery selling bread and viennoiserie		
		œuf	egg
brioche	a soft, sweet bread made with eggs and butter	*pain*	bread – choose from a rich variety of flavoured breads as well as the traditional baguette
casse-croûte	literally 'to break a crust' – a snack		
une crêpe	pancake served with various fillings	*pain au chocolat*	similar to a croissant, but pillow shaped and filled with chocolate
croque-monsieur	grilled ham and cheese sandwich		
croque-madame	as above but topped with a fried egg	*pâte*	pastry or dough, not to be confused with pâtes, which is pasta or pâté, the meat terrine
crudités	raw vegetables served sliced or diced with a dressing, as a starter or sandwich filling		
		riz	rice
		rouille	saffron, garlic and paprika mayonnaise, served with soupe de poisson and bouillabaisse
en croûte	food cooked in a pastry parcel		
escargots	snails		
forestière	generally sautéed with mushrooms	*salade verte*	simple green salad with vinaigrette dressing
fromage	cheese		
fromage de chèvre	goat's milk cheese	*soupe/potage*	soup
galette	savoury filled pancake made with buckwheat flour, served as a starter or main course	*viennoiserie*	baked items such as croissants and brioches

Index

Titles available in the Footprint *Focus* range

Latin America	UK RRP	US RRP
Bahia & Salvador	£7.99	$11.95
Brazilian Amazon	£7.99	$11.95
Brazilian Pantanal	£6.99	$9.95
Buenos Aires & Pampas	£7.99	$11.95
Cartagena & Caribbean Coast	£7.99	$11.95
Costa Rica	£8.99	$12.95
Cuzco, La Paz & Lake Titicaca	£8.99	$12.95
El Salvador	£5.99	$8.95
Guadalajara & Pacific Coast	£6.99	$9.95
Guatemala	£8.99	$12.95
Guyana, Guyane & Surinam	£5.99	$8.95
Havana	£6.99	$9.95
Honduras	£7.99	$11.95
Nicaragua	£7.99	$11.95
Northeast Argentina & Uruguay	£8.99	$12.95
Paraguay	£5.99	$8.95
Quito & Galápagos Islands	£7.99	$11.95
Recife & Northeast Brazil	£7.99	$11.95
Rio de Janeiro	£8.99	$12.95
São Paulo	£5.99	$8.95
Uruguay	£6.99	$9.95
Venezuela	£8.99	$12.95
Yucatán Peninsula	£6.99	$9.95

Asia	UK RRP	US RRP
Angkor Wat	£5.99	$8.95
Bali & Lombok	£8.99	$12.95
Chennai & Tamil Nadu	£8.99	$12.95
Chiang Mai & Northern Thailand	£7.99	$11.95
Goa	£6.99	$9.95
Gulf of Thailand	£8.99	$12.95
Hanoi & Northern Vietnam	£8.99	$12.95
Ho Chi Minh City & Mekong Delta	£7.99	$11.95
Java	£7.99	$11.95
Kerala	£7.99	$11.95
Kolkata & West Bengal	£5.99	$8.95
Mumbai & Gujarat	£8.99	$12.95

Africa & Middle East	UK RRP	US RRP
Beirut	£6.99	$9.95
Cairo & Nile Delta	£8.99	$12.95
Damascus	£5.99	$8.95
Durban & KwaZulu Natal	£8.99	$12.95
Fès & Northern Morocco	£8.99	$12.95
Jerusalem	£8.99	$12.95
Johannesburg & Kruger National Park	£7.99	$1
Kenya's Beaches	£8.99	$1
Kilimanjaro & Northern Tanzania	£8.99	$1
Luxor to Aswan	£8.99	$1
Nairobi & Rift Valley	£7.99	$1
Red Sea & Sinai	£7.99	$1
Zanzibar & Pemba	£7.99	$1

Europe	UK RRP	U
Bilbao & Basque Region	£6.99	$9
Brittany West Coast	£7.99	$1
Cádiz & Costa de la Luz	£6.99	$9
Granada & Sierra Nevada	£6.99	$9
Languedoc: Carcassonne to Montpellier	£7.99	$11.95
Málaga	£5.99	$8.95
Marseille & Western Provence	£7.99	$11.95
Orkney & Shetland Islands	£5.99	$8.95
Santander & Picos de Europa	£7.99	$11.95
Sardinia: Alghero & the North	£7.99	$11.95
Sardinia: Cagliari & the South	£7.99	$11.95
Seville	£5.99	$8.95
Sicily: Palermo & the Northwest	£7.99	$11.95
Sicily: Catania & the Southeast	£7.99	$11.95
Siena & Southern Tuscany	£7.99	$11.95
Sorrento, Capri & Amalfi Coast	£6.99	$9.95
Skye & Outer Hebrides	£6.99	$9.95
Verona & Lake Garda	£7.99	$11.95

North America	UK RRP	US RRP
Vancouver & Rockies	£8.99	$12.95

Australasia	UK RRP	US RRP
Brisbane & Queensland	£8.99	$12.95
Perth	£7.99	$11.95

For the latest books, e-books and a wealth of travel information, visit us at:

www.footprinttravelgu[ide] ... [chec]k for the latest ... [produc]t releases, offers ... [comp]etitions: ... [.com]/footprintbooks.